Christmas *with* Possibilities

16 QUILTED HOLIDAY PROJECTS

LYNDA MILLIGAN & NANCY SMITH

C&T PUBLISHING

Publisher: Amy Marson

Creative Director: Gailen Runge

Acquisitions Editor: Susanne Woods

Editor: Lynn Koolish

Proofreader: Wordfirm Inc.

Cover Designer: Kristy Zacharias

Book Designer: Christina D. Jarumay

Production Coordinators: Casey Dukes and Kirstie L. Pettersen

Production Editor: Julia Cianci

Photography by Brad Bartholomew unless otherwise noted

Published by C&T Publishing, Inc., P.O. Box 1456, Lafayette, CA 94549

Library of Congress Cataloging-in-Publication Data

Milligan, Lynda, 1951-

Christmas with possibilities : 16 quilted holiday projects / Lynda Milligan and Nancy Smith.

p. cm.

ISBN 978-1-57120-939-9 (soft cover)

1. Patchwork--Patterns. 2. Quilting--Patterns. 3. Christmas decorations. I. Smith, Nancy, 1943 Oct. 17- II. Title.

TT835.M53152 2010

746.46'041--dc22

2009038059

Printed in China

10 9 8 7 6 5 4 3 2 1

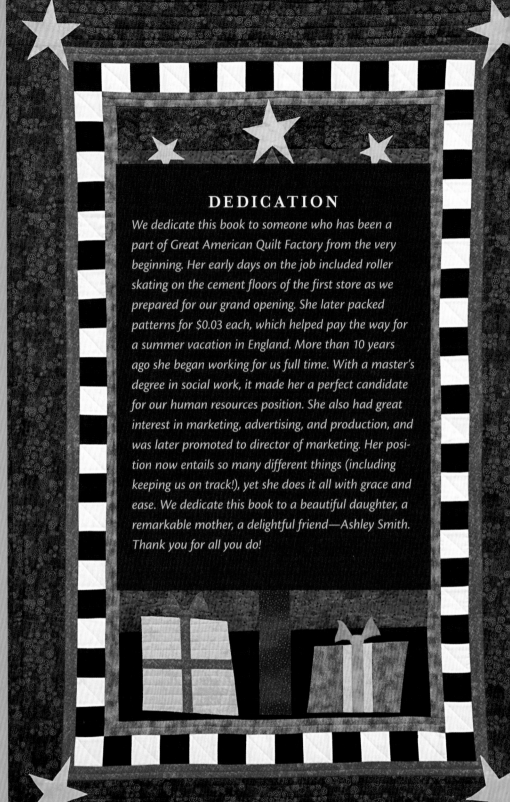

DEDICATION

We dedicate this book to someone who has been a part of Great American Quilt Factory from the very beginning. Her early days on the job included roller skating on the cement floors of the first store as we prepared for our grand opening. She later packed patterns for $0.03 each, which helped pay the way for a summer vacation in England. More than 10 years ago she began working for us full time. With a master's degree in social work, it made her a perfect candidate for our human resources position. She also had great interest in marketing, advertising, and production, and was later promoted to director of marketing. Her position now entails so many different things (including keeping us on track!), yet she does it all with grace and ease. We dedicate this book to a beautiful daughter, a remarkable mother, a delightful friend—Ashley Smith. Thank you for all you do!

ACKNOWLEDGMENTS

We want to thank the many people who helped to create this delightful book. First of all, we thank everyone who was a part of the first Joy to the World book, which was a tremendous success. Second, we thank C&T Publishing for partnering with us and helping to bring these favorite projects back to life. Finally, we give heartfelt appreciation to our creative staff for designing terrific new projects from fresh ideas. As a team we create fun and inspiring books that we can all be proud of.

Contents

INTRODUCTION

Thank you for bringing us into your home for the holiday season! We know you will find the projects here to be fun, cozy, and perfect for decorating your home or giving as holiday gifts. There is something here for everyone, whether you're looking to make a project to celebrate the Christmas season or you want to make a quilt that will last all winter long. Either way, all you need to do is add a little love of your own, and you can easily create beautiful quilts, wallhangings, album covers, and so much more. Enjoy!

Bear's Paw
quilt

BEAR'S PAW
QUILT

Finished block size: 10½″ × 10½″

Finished quilt size: 67″ × 91″

Materials and Yardage

Yardage is based on fabric that is at least 42″ wide.

- **Darks:** (assorted reds): 24 fat quarters or ¼ yard pieces

- **Light** (white): 6¼ yards

- **Backing:** 5¾ yards

- **Binding:** ¾ yard

- **Batting:** 73″ × 97″

Cutting

When strips appear in the cutting list, cut crossgrain strips (selvage to selvage).

DARK (ASSORTED REDS)
For each block: (use only 1 red per block):

Claws: 8 squares 2⅜″ × 2⅜″, cut each in half diagonally

Paws: 4 squares 3½″ × 3½″

Center: 1 square 2″ × 2″

Border 2: 96 squares (4 of each fabric) 2⅜″ × 2⅜″, cut each in half diagonally

LIGHT (WHITE)
For each block:

Claw units: 8 squares 2⅜″ × 2⅜″, cut each in half diagonally

Sides: 4 rectangles 2″ × 5″

Corners: 4 squares 2″ × 2″

Sashing: 35 squares 2″ × 2″ and 58 rectangles 2″ × 11″

Border 1: 8 strips 5¾″ wide

Border 2: 96 squares 2⅜″ × 2⅜″, cut each in half diagonally and 4 squares 2″ × 2″

Border 3: 9 strips 2½″ wide

Binding: 9 strips 2½″ wide

Directions
Use ¼″ seam allowance unless otherwise noted.

QUILT CENTER

1. Make 24 blocks following the diagram below. Press.

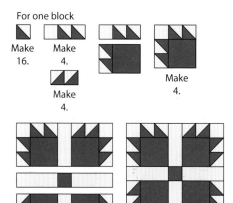

Block construction

2. Make 7 sashing rows with 4 sashing rectangles and 5 sashing squares.

3. Make 6 block rows with 4 blocks and 5 sashing rectangles.

4. Stitch the rows together. Press well.

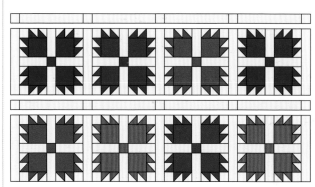

Row construction

BORDER 1

Measure the length of the quilt. Piece the border strips to the measured length, and stitch them to the sides of the quilt. Repeat at the top and the bottom. Press.

BORDER 2

1. Make 192 half-square triangle units using the various darks with the light.

2. Stitch 56 units together for each side of the quilt, reversing the order at the center as shown in the Quilt Assembly Diagram. Stitch the units together with a scant ¼" seam allowance. Press well.

3. Lay the border edge to edge with the quilt and adjust the borders to fit by making a few seams between the units a bit deeper or shallower. Repeat for the other side border. Stitch the side borders to the quilt.

4. Repeat for the top and bottom borders using 40 units for each, adding the 2" light squares at each end. Press.

BORDER 3

Add Border 3 in the same manner as Border 1. Press.

FINISHING

1. Piece the backing so it is the same size as the batting.

2. Layer, baste, and quilt.

3. Trim the backing and batting to the same size as the quilt top.

4. Bind the quilt using a ⅜" seam allowance (see page 78).

Quilt Assembly Diagram

Holly Berry Log Cabin
quilt

HOLLY BERRY LOG CABIN QUILT

Finished block size: 16½" × 16½"

Finished size: 66" × 66"

Materials and Yardage

Yardage is based on fabric that is at least 42" wide.

- **Lights:** Assorted whites to total 4 yards
- **Darks:** Assorted reds & greens to total 4 yards
- **Leaves:** Assorted greens to total 1½ yards
- **Berries:** ⅛ yard
- **Backing:** 4¼ yards
- **Binding:** ⅝ yard
- **Batting:** 72" × 72"
- **Fusible web**

Cutting

Lights

Piece 1: 16 squares 2" × 2"

Piece 2: 16 rectangles 2" × 3½"

Piece 5: 16 rectangles 2" × 5"

Piece 6: 16 rectangles 2" × 6½"

Piece 9: 16 rectangles 2" × 8"

Piece 10: 16 rectangles 2" × 9½"

Piece 13: 16 rectangles 2" × 11"

Piece 14: 16 rectangles 2" × 12½"

Piece 17: 16 rectangles 2" × 14"

Piece 18: 16 rectangles 2" × 15½"

Darks

Centers: 16 squares 2" × 2"

Piece 3: 16 rectangles 2" × 3½"

Piece 4: 16 rectangles 2" × 5"

Piece 7: 16 rectangles 2" × 6½"

Piece 8: 16 rectangles 2" × 8"

Piece 11: 16 rectangles 2" × 9½"

Piece 12: 16 rectangles 2" × 11"

Piece 15: 16 rectangles 2" × 12½"

Piece 16: 16 rectangles 2" × 14"

Piece 19: 16 rectangles 2" × 15½"

Piece 20: 16 rectangles 2" × 17"

Binding: 7 strips 2½" wide

Cut appliqué as needed: (Patterns are on page 10):
38 holly leaves, 11 maple leaves, 8 oak leaves, and 63 berries.

Directions

Use ¼" seam allowance unless otherwise noted.

See pages 73–74 for appliqué instructions.

MAKE THE QUILT TOP

1. Make 16 blocks in 5 counterclockwise rounds, placing the fabrics randomly. Press the blocks.

Round 1

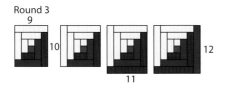

Round 2

Round 3

Round 4

Round 5

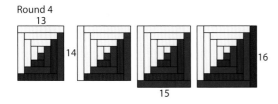

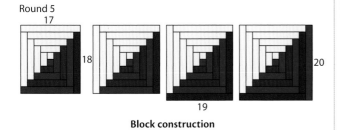

Block construction

2. Make 4 rows of 4 blocks, arranging the blocks as shown. Stitch the rows together. Press.

3. Appliqué the leaves and berries on the light sections.

FINISHING

1. Piece the backing so it is the same size as the batting.

2. Layer, baste, and quilt.

3. Trim the backing and batting to the same size as the quilt top.

4. Bind the quilt using a ⅜" seam allowance (see page 78).

Quilt Assembly Diagram

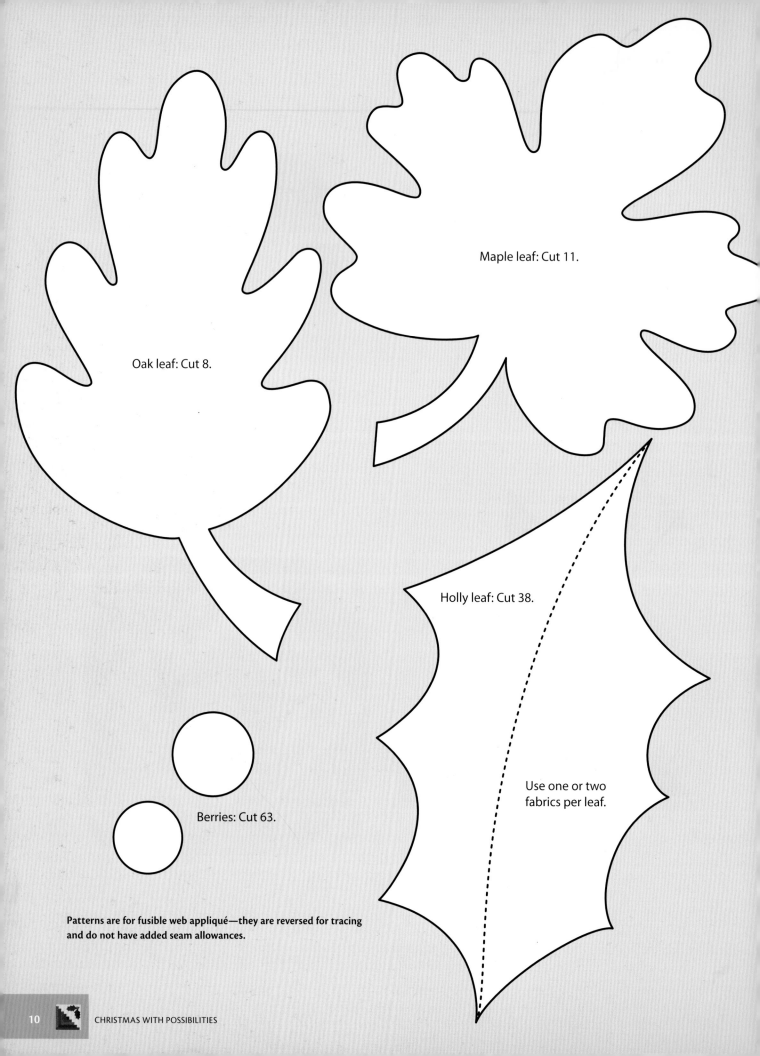

Maple leaf: Cut 11.

Oak leaf: Cut 8.

Holly leaf: Cut 38.

Use one or two
fabrics per leaf.

Berries: Cut 63.

Patterns are for fusible web appliqué—they are reversed for tracing
and do not have added seam allowances.

Three Tall Santas
quilt

Photo by C&T Publishing

THREE TALL SANTAS QUILT

Finished quilt size: 58″ × 64″

Materials and Yardage

Yardage is based on fabric that is at least 42" wide.

- **Assorted reds:** to total 1 yard
- **Assorted greens:** to total 1 yard
- **Assorted golds:** to total ¾ yard
- **Background for Santas:** ⅝ yard
- **Background for all star blocks:** 1 yard
- **White for snow:** ¼ yard
- **Black for lightbulb bases:** ⅛ yard
- **Scraps for appliqué:** up to 4″ × 8″
- **Narrow stripe for Borders 1 and 3:** 1⅝ yards
- **Red and white for Border 4:** ½ yard each
- **Border 5:** 1½ yards
- **Backing:** 3⅞ yards
- **Binding:** ⅝ yard
- **Batting:** 64″ × 70″
- **Green fusible bias tape:** 7 yards

Cutting

When strips appear in the cutting list, cut crossgrain strips (selvage to selvage), except as noted.

Background for Santas: 18½″ × 24½″

Snow: 5½″ × 18½″

Border 1 (cut on lengthwise grain; measurements below include extra length for mitering):

  2 strips 3½″ × 27″

  2 strips 3½″ × 33″

Border 2 (cutting is for one 6″ block):

Use two fabrics for each star and the same background for all. Cut 8 red, 8 green, and 6 gold blocks.

  Star fabric #1 center: 1 square 3½″ × 3½″

  Star fabric #2 points: 4 squares 2⅜″ × 2⅜″, cut each in half diagonally

  Background: 4 squares 2⅜″ × 2⅜″, cut each in half diagonally

  Background corners: 4 squares 2″ × 2″

Border 3 (cut on *lengthwise* grain— extra length is included for mitering): 2 strips 3½″ × 44″ and 2 strips 3½″ × 50″

Border 4:

  45 squares each of Border 4 fabric 2⅞″ × 2⅞″, cut each in half diagonally

  White corners: 4 squares 2½″ × 2½″

Border 5: 7 strips 6½″ wide

Binding: 7 strips 2½″ wide

Cut appliqué as needed: (Patterns are on pages 70–71): 3 Santas, 52 lightbulbs, 12 holly leaves, and 12 berries. *Note: Enlarge Santas and star 200%.*

Directions

Use ¼″ seam allowance unless otherwise noted.

See pages 73–74 for appliqué instructions.

QUILT CENTER

1. Trim the top of the snow piece with a gentle curve, and appliqué it to the Santa background.

2. Stitch the Border 1 strips to the background, centering them from end to end. Stop stitching at the seam intersections. Miter each corner (pages 75–76). Press.

3. Appliqué the Santas. The star and right Santa's hat are overlapped onto Border 1.

BORDERS 2 AND 3

1. Make 22 blocks for Border 2. Press.

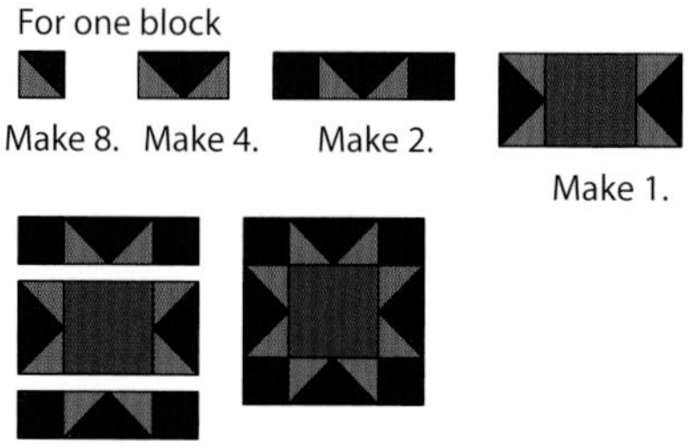

For one block

Make 8.　Make 4.　Make 2.　Make 1.

Border 2 blocks

2. Place the blocks around the Santa center, distributing the colors as desired. Stitch together the 5 blocks for each side border, and then stitch the borders to the quilt. Repeat with the 6 blocks for the top and bottom.

3. Repeat Quilt Center Step 2 for Border 3.

BORDER 4

1. Make 90 half-square triangle units (page 73).

Make 90.

2. Make 2 identical side borders of 24 units each.

Make 2.

3. Make 2 identical borders for the top and bottom using 21 half-square triangle units with squares at each end.

Make 2.

4. Stitch the side borders to the quilt using the Quilt Assembly Diagram as a guide for the direction of the red triangles.

5. Stitch the top and bottom borders to the quilt using the Quilt Assembly Diagram as a guide for the direction of the red triangles.

BORDER 5

1. Press the quilt well. Measure the length of the quilt. Piece the border strips to the measured length, and stitch the borders to the sides of the quilt. Repeat at the top and bottom. Press.

2. Cut a piece of fusible bias tape the width of the quilt. Pin the bias tape

to the bottom border of the quilt. Start at the center and work toward a corner, curving one end of the bias tape slightly down and then back up, keeping the top of the "up curve" even with the seam between Borders 3 and 4. Trim the end of the tape at the center of the corner where it will be covered by the holly leaves. Repeat at the other end. Press the bias tape to the quilt. Repeat for the other 3 sides of the quilt. The curve will be gentler on the sides of the quilt.

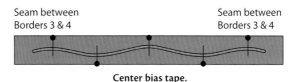

Seam between
Borders 3 & 4   Seam between
Borders 3 & 4

Center bias tape.

3. Distribute the bulbs along the bias tape. Cover the ends of the bias tape with 3 holly leaves and 3 berries. Appliqué everything in place.

FINISHING

1. Piece the backing so it is the same size as the batting.

2. Layer, baste, and quilt.

3. Trim the backing and batting to the same size as the quilt top.

4. Bind the quilt using a ⅜" seam allowance (see page 78).

Quilt Assembly Diagram

Christmas Houses
quilt

CHRISTMAS HOUSES
QUILT

Finished block size: 14″ × 14″

Finished quilt size: 78″ × 78″

Materials and Yardage

Yardage is based on fabric that is at least 42″ wide.

- **Large scraps for sky and ground:** enough for 16 blocks
- **Medium and small scraps for appliqué**
- **Sashing rectangles:** 1⅝ yards
- **Sashing squares:** ¼ yard
- **Border:** 1¾ yards
- **Backing:** 5 yards
- **Binding:** ⅔ yard
- **Batting:** 84″ × 84″

Cutting

When strips appear in the cutting list, cut crossgrain strips (selvage to selvage).

Sashing rectangles: 40 rectangles 2½″ × 14½″

Sashing squares: 25 squares 2½″ × 2½″

Border: 8 strips 6½″ wide

Binding: 8 strips 2½″ wide

Cut appliqué as needed (Patterns are on page 16.)

Directions

Use ¼″ seam allowance unless otherwise noted.

See pages 73–74 for appliqué instructions.

HOUSE BLOCKS

1. Sky and ground can be 2 rectangles sewn together, or they can be made with appliqué pieces (hills, snow, and so on) overlapping on a sky square. Blocks should be 14½″ × 14½″, including seam allowances, to finish at 14″ × 14″.

2. Make 5 sashing rows with 4 rectangles and 5 squares.

3. Make block rows with 4 blocks and 5 sashing rectangles.

4. Stitch the rows together. Press.

BORDER

1. Measure the length of the quilt. Piece border strips to the measured length, and stitch them to the sides of the quilt. Repeat at the top and bottom. Press.

2. If desired, appliqué stars overlapping the borders.

FINISHING

1. Piece the backing so it is the same size as the batting.

2. Layer, baste, and quilt.

3. Trim the backing and batting to the same size as the quilt top.

4. Bind the quilt using a ⅜″ seam allowance (see page 78).

> ★ *This is a great project for a group quilt or a block exchange: Everyone gets the pattern pieces and can customize their house by making the house taller or shorter, changing the windows, using the shed or not.*

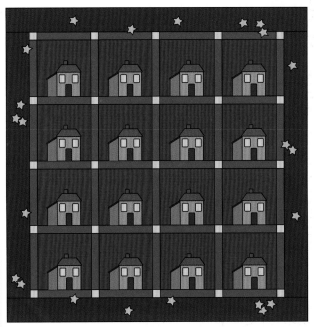

Quilt Assembly Diagram

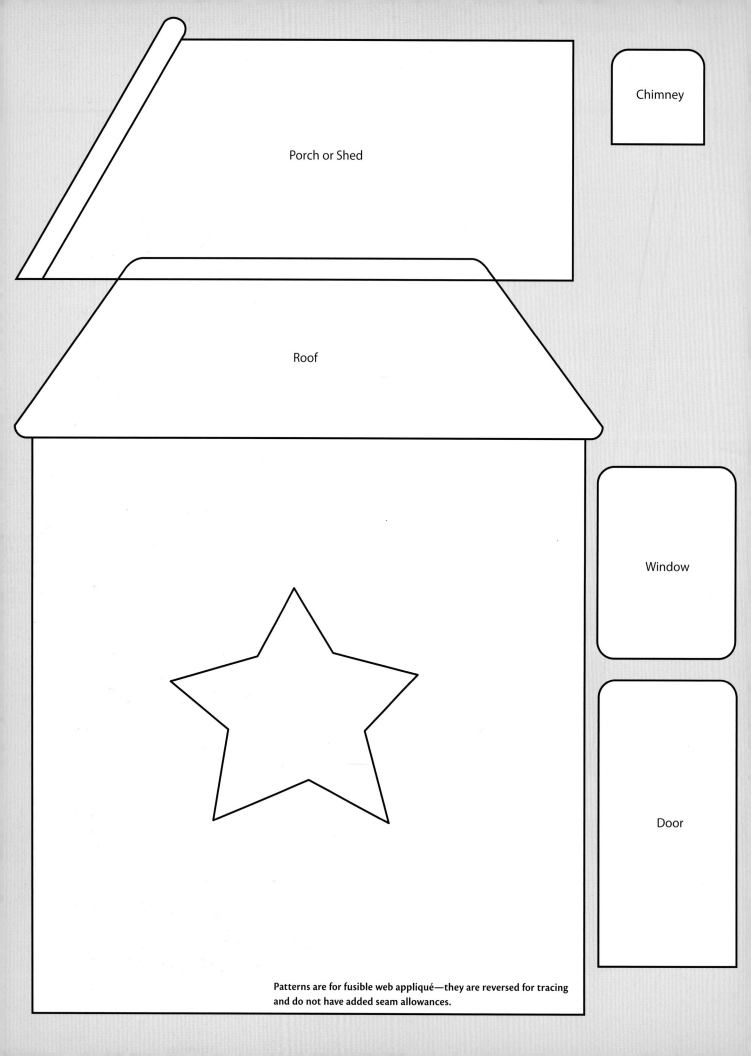

Porch or Shed

Chimney

Roof

Window

Door

Patterns are for fusible web appliqué—they are reversed for tracing and do not have added seam allowances.

Starry Starry Night
quilt

Photo by C&T Publishing

STARRY STARRY NIGHT
QUILT

Finished block size: 10″ × 10″

Finished quilt size: 57″ × 70″

Materials and Yardage

Yardage is based on fabric that is at least 42″ wide.

- **Assorted reds:** ⅓ yard each of 18 or more
- **Golds:** ¼ yard each of 18 or more
- **Border 1:** ⅜ yard green
- **Border 2:** ⅝ yard medium red
- **Border 2:** ¾ yard dark red
- **Binding:** ⅝ yard
- **Backing:** 3¾ yards
- **Batting:** 63″ × 76″

Cutting

When strips appear in the cutting list, cut crossgrain strips (selvage to selvage).

Assorted reds: 31 pieces 3½″ × 10½″ and 12 squares 3½″ × 3½″ for sashing; the remaining fabric is for paper piecing large stars

Golds: 96 squares 2″ × 2″ for small stars; the remaining fabric is for paper piecing large stars

Border 1 (green): 6 strips 1½″ wide

Border 2:

> **Medium red:** 36 squares 3⅞″ × 3⅞″, cut each in half diagonally

> **Dark red:** 6 squares 3½″ × 3½″, 2 pieces 3½″ × 4½″, 36 squares 3⅞″ × 3⅞″; cut each 3⅞″ square in half diagonally

Binding: 7 strips 2¼″ wide

Directions

Use ¼″ seam allowance unless otherwise noted.

ASSEMBLE THE QUILT TOP
Paper-piecing patterns are on pages 19–21.

1. Paper piece (pages 74–75) 20 blocks as shown.

Make 20.

2. Make sashing units by stitching the gold squares to the corners of the red rectangles. If desired, trim the seam allowance to ¼″. Press.

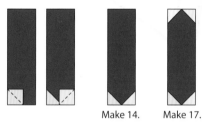

Make 14. Make 17.

Make sashing units.

3. Arrange the blocks and sashing. Stitch them into horizontal rows. Stitch the rows together. Press.

4. For Border 1: Make 2 side borders by piecing strips to the same length as the quilt. Stitch the borders to the quilt. Press. Repeat at the top and bottom.

5. For border 2: Make 72 half-square triangle units (page 73). Press. Stitch them into 2 side and 2 top/bottom borders using the dark red 3½″ squares at the center and ends of the top and bottom borders, and the 3½″ × 4½″ rectangles at the center of the side borders. Adjust the borders to fit at the center square or rectangle. Press. Stitch the side borders to the quilt. Press. Repeat for the top and bottom.

Make 72.

Sides—Make 2.

Top and bottom—Make 2.

FINISHING

1. Piece the backing so it is the same size as the batting.

2. Layer, baste, and quilt.

3. Trim the backing and batting to the same size as the quilt top.

4. Bind the quilt using a ¼" seam allowance (see page 78).

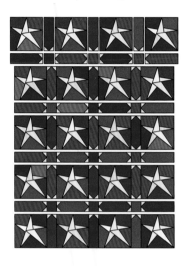

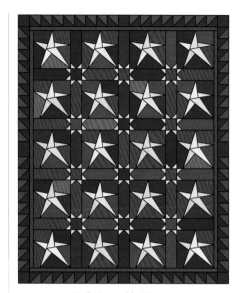

Quilt Assembly Diagram

3

2

1

Pattern has been reversed for paper piecing.

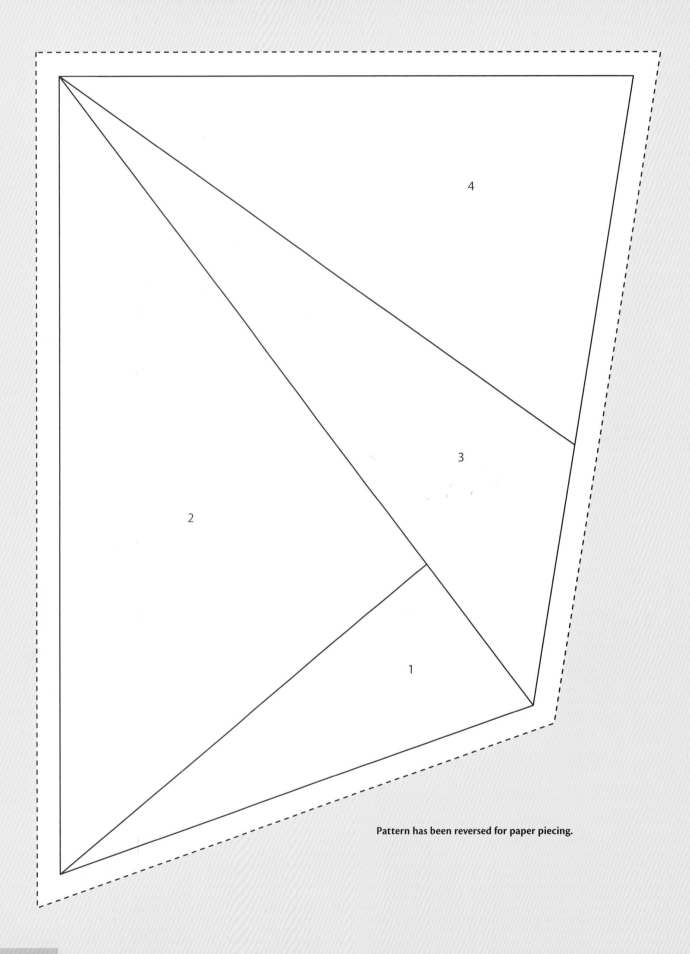

4

3

2

1

Pattern has been reversed for paper piecing.

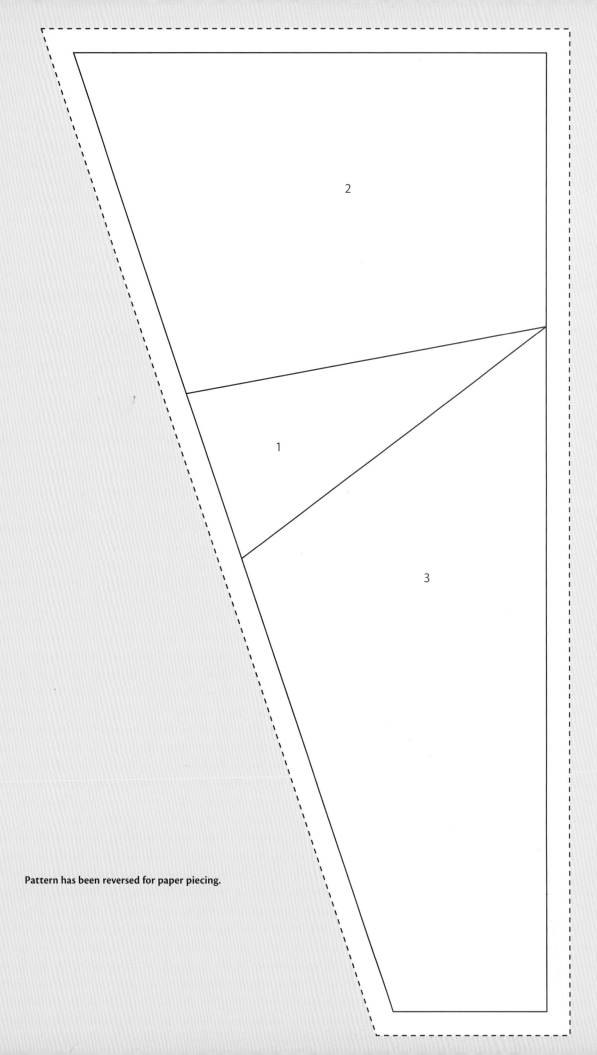

Pattern has been reversed for paper piecing.

Strippy Trees
quilt

STRIPPY TREES QUILT

Finished block size: 8″ × 10″ and 4″ × 5″

Finished quilt size: 50″ × 66″

Materials and Yardage

Yardage is based on fabric that is at least 42″ wide.

- **Trees:**

  ⅔ yard each of 10 medium and dark greens

  ⅛ yard each dark pink and dark purple

- **Backgrounds:** ½ yard each of 4 light blues, 2 light greens, 2 light golds, 2 medium purples, and 1 medium pink

- **Trunks:** ¼ yard brown

- **Border 1:** ⅜ yard dark pink

- **Border 2:** ⅝ yard green

- **Binding:** ⅝ yard

- **Backing:** 3⅜ yards

- **Batting:** 56″ × 72″

Cutting

When strips appear in the cutting list, cut crossgrain strips (selvage to selvage).

Trees

Green: 1½″–2½″ strips in ¼″ increments; start with 1 strip of each width of each fabric; the remaining fabric is for plain sides of big trees and both sides of small trees

Pink and purple: start with 1 strip 1″ wide and 1 strip 1½″ wide of each

Backgrounds

Blue: use for paper piecing small trees

Other colors: for 2 large blocks cut 2 pieces 5½″ × 11″; place right sides together; cut in half diagonally (use for paper piecing); cut 4 pieces 2½″ × 4″ for trunk units

Trunks: 24 pieces 1½″ × 2½″ for large tree trunk units (trunk units of large trees are not paper pieced); remaining fabric is for paper piecing small trees

Border 1: 6 strips 1½″ wide

Border 2: 6 strips 2½″ wide

Binding: 7 strips 2½″ wide

Directions

Use ¼″ seam allowance unless otherwise noted.

BLOCKS

Make 36 copies of the paper-piecing pattern on page 27. Make 1 copy each of the paper-piecing patterns on pages 25–26; tape the halves together, and then make 24 copies of the full-sized pattern.

BLOCK A

Paper piece (pages 74–75) 36 blocks using light blues for the background.

Paper piece 36 blocks.

BLOCK B

1. Trace the diagonal tree lines to the wrong side of 10 patterns.

2. String piece the full center section on the traced side of the pattern. Slant the strips as desired.

3. Paper piece the background triangles to the unit using light greens, golds, purples, and pinks.

4. Piece 10 trunk units. Stitch the trunk units to the top units. Press.

 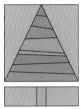 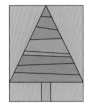

String piece tree, and add trunk.

BLOCK C

1. Trace the diagonal and center vertical tree lines to the wrong side of 14 patterns.

2. String piece the tree units on the traced side, covering half of the center section—sometimes left side, sometimes right. Slant strips as desired.

3. Paper piece the plain side of the tree with greens, then piece the backgrounds using light greens, golds, pinks, and purples.

4. Piece 14 trunk units. Stitch the trunk units to the top units. Press.

 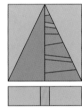 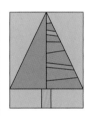

String piece tree, and add trunk.

ASSEMBLE THE QUILT TOP

1. Arrange the blocks. Stitch the blocks into horizontal rows. Stitch the rows together. Press.

2. To make Border 1: Make 2 side borders by piecing strips to the same length as the quilt. Stitch them to the quilt. Press. Repeat for the top and bottom.

3. To make Border 2: Repeat Step 2.

FINISHING

1. Piece the backing so it is the same size as the batting.

2. Layer, baste, and quilt.

3. Trim the backing and batting to the same size as the quilt top.

4. Bind the quilt using a ⅜" seam allowance (see page 78).

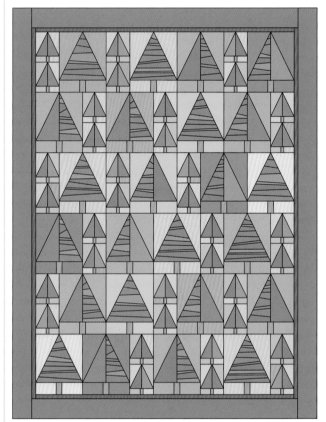

Quilt Assembly Diagram

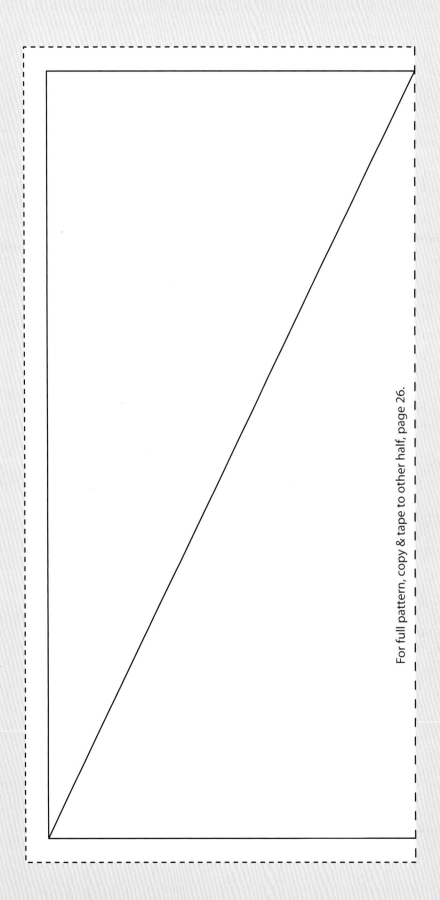

For full pattern, copy & tape to other half, page 26.

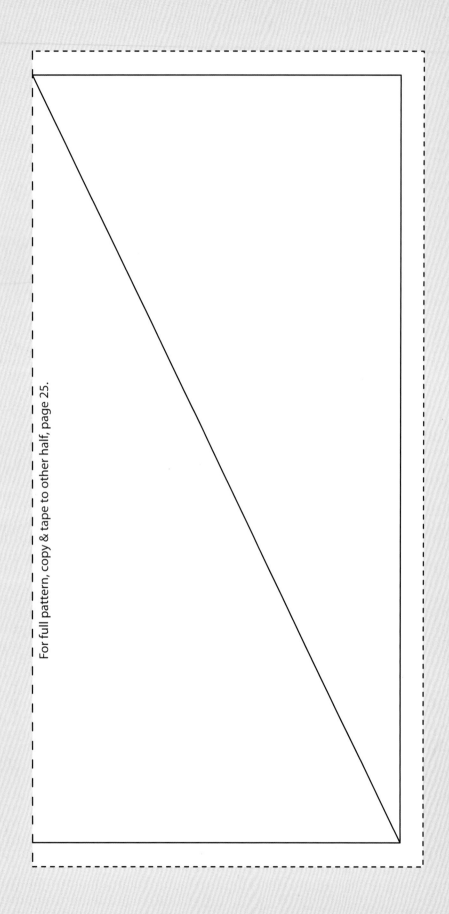

For full pattern, copy & tape to other half, page 25.

CHRISTMAS WITH POSSIBILITIES

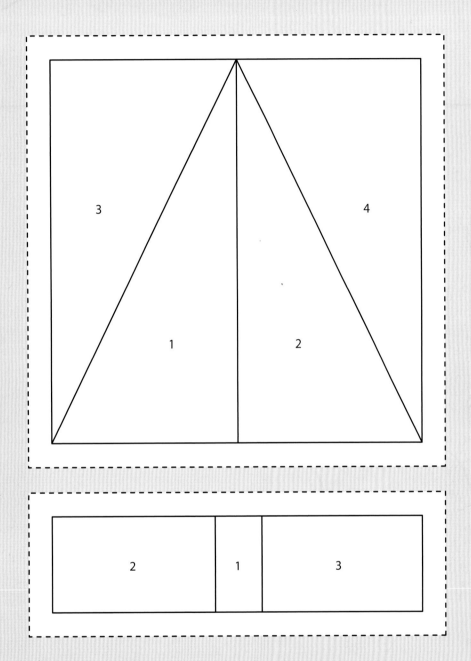

Deck the Halls
quilt

CHRISTMAS WITH POSSIBILITIES

DECK THE HALLS QUILT

Finished block size: 12″ × 12″

Finished quilt size: 50″ × 62″

Materials and Yardage

Yardage is based on fabric that is at least 42″ wide.

- **Background and sashing:** 1 yard black
- **Sashing:** ¼ yard black-and-white lengthwise stripe
- **Sashing and appliqué:** ⅜ yard each of 1 green, 2 pinks, 2 yellows, 2 oranges, 2 reds, 2 purples, and 2 blues

  ⅜ yard pink (border ribbons)
- **Borders 1 and 2:** ½ yard purple
- **Borders 2 and 3:** 1⅛ yards black, ⅓ yard each pink and orange
- **Border 4:** ½ yard black-and-white lengthwise stripe
- **Binding:** ⅝ yard
- **Backing:** 3⅜ yards
- **Batting:** 56″ × 68″
- **Fusible web**

Cutting

When strips appear in the cutting list, cut crossgrain strips (selvage to selvage).

Background and sashing (black):

12 squares 9½″ × 9½″

12 squares 1½″ × 1½″

Sashing (stripe): 12 pieces 1½″ × 9½″

Sashing (colors):

24 pieces total 1½″ × 9½″ in pairs for the sides of vertical units

12 pieces total 1″ × 12½″ for the tops of horizontal units

12 pieces total 2″ × 12½″ for the bottoms of horizontal units

12 pieces total 1½″ × 10½″ in pairs and 12 pieces total 1½″ × 1½″ in pairs (for centers of horizontal units)

Borders 1 and 2 (purple):

5 strips 1½″ wide

2 squares 2⅞″ × 2⅞″, cut each in half diagonally

Border 2 (black):

44 squares 2⅞″ × 2⅞″, cut each in half diagonally

4 squares 2½″ × 2½″

Border 2 (pink & orange): 21 squares 2⅞″ × 2⅞″, cut each in half diagonally

Border 3 (black): 6 strips 3½″ wide

Border 4 (stripe): 6 strips 1¾″ wide

Binding: 7 strips 2½″ wide

Cut appliqué as needed: (Patterns are on pages 31–32): 3 round and 2 pointed ornaments, 6 small stars for each round ornament, 4 large stars and spirals, 3 hearts and 9 holly leaves, 7 hangers, 5 ornament tops, and 4 border ribbons.

Directions

Use ¼″ seam allowance unless otherwise noted.

See pages 73–74 for appliqué instructions.

BLOCKS

1. Make 12 vertical sashing units with a pair of colored pieces on either side of a stripe piece. Press.

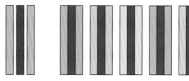

Make 12.

2. Make 12 horizontal sashing units using the remaining sashing pieces. Make some with mostly warm colors and some with mostly cool colors, if desired. Press.

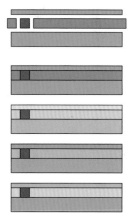

Make 12.

3. Stitch the vertical units to the left sides of the background squares. Press. Stitch the horizontal units to the bottoms of the background squares. Press.

4. Appliqué the ornaments to the blocks.

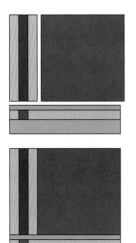

Make 12.

ASSEMBLE THE QUILT TOP

1. Arrange the blocks, and stitch them into horizontal rows. Stitch the rows together. Press.

2. For Border 1: Make 2 side borders by piecing strips to the same length as the quilt. Stitch the side borders to the quilt. Press. Repeat at the top and bottom.

3. For Border 2: Make 42 half-square triangle units (page 73) with black and orange. Make 42 half-square triangle units with black and pink. Make 4 half-square triangle units with black and purple. Press. Stitch them together for the borders as shown in the Quilt Assembly Diagram. Note the plain black squares placed at the center of each border. Press the borders, and stitch the side borders to the quilt. Press. Repeat with the top and bottom borders.

Right side border—Make 1.

Left side border—Make 1.

Top and bottom borders—Make 2.

4. For Border 3: Repeat Step 2. Appliqué ribbons to each border, centered side to side and end to end. Press.

5. For Border 4: Repeat Step 2.

FINISHING

1. Piece the backing so it is the same size as the batting.

2. Layer, baste, and quilt.

3. Trim the backing and batting to the same size as the quilt top.

4. Bind the quilt using a ⅜" seam allowance (see page 78).

> ★ To make three pillows, use colored fabric leftovers from the quilt. Purchase ⅜ yard background fabric, two yards for envelope backings, and three 16" × 16" pillow forms. If you want to quilt the pillow top, you'll need batting and backing. Make the blocks as described for the quilt, then add two borders with finished widths of ½" and 1½".

Quilt Assembly Diagram

Match
dashed
lines.

For full pattern, tape together 3 center
segments & 2 end segments (1 & 1 reversed).

Patterns are for fusible web
appliqué—they are reversed for
tracing and do not have added
seam allowances.

Match
dashed
lines.

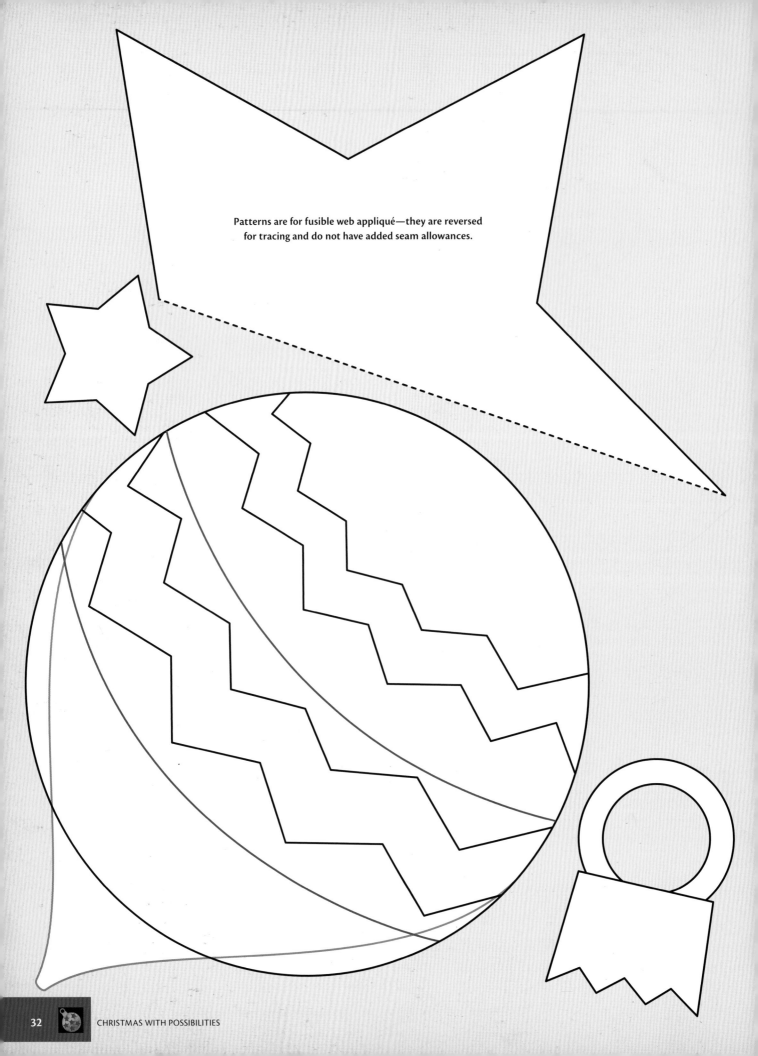

Patterns are for fusible web appliqué—they are reversed
for tracing and do not have added seam allowances.

Advent Calendar
wallhanging

ADVENT CALENDAR
WALLHANGING

Finished quilt size: 38″ × 58″

Materials and Yardage

Yardage is based on fabric that is at least 42″ wide.

- **Center background:**

  ⅔ yard medium blue

  ⅔ yard dark blue

  ¼ yard black

- **Tree:**

  ¼ yard each of 6 greens

  ⅛ yard brown

- **Stars:** ⅙ yard yellow or gold

- **Gifts:**

  ¼ yard each yellow and purple

  ⅛ yard each red, orange and yellow

- **Ornaments:** ⅛ yard each of 5 fabrics

- **Border 1:** ¼ yard purple

- **Border 2:** ¼ yard each of black and white

- **Border 3:** ¼ yard red

- **Border 4:** ⅞ yard blue

- **Binding:** ½ yard

- **Backing:** 2 yards

- **Batting:** 42″ × 62″

- **Ornaments:** ⅜ yard craft-weight interfacing with fusible on both sides, such as fast2fuse

- **⅛″ ribbon:** 1½ yards

- **Small buttons or bells:** 24

- **Fusible web**

Cutting

When strips appear in the cutting list, cut crossgrain strips (selvage to selvage).

Center background

Medium blue:

  1 piece 3½″ × 22½″ (bottom blue row)

  3 pieces 5½″ × 22½″ (#1, #3, #5)

Dark blue:

  1 piece 3½″ × 22½″ (top blue row)

  3 pieces 5½″ × 22½″ (#2, #4, #6)

Black: 1 piece 6½″ × 22½″

Ornaments

  48 squares 3″ × 3″ in sets of 2 of same color for each ornament (front and backing)

  24 squares 3″ × 3″ of fusible craft-weight interfacing

Border 1: 4 strips 1½″ wide

Border 2: 36 squares of each fabric 2½″ × 2½″

Border 3: 4 strips 1½″ wide

Border 4: 5 strips 4½″ wide

Binding: 5 strips 2½″ wide

Cut appliqué as needed Patterns are on pages 37–39 for gifts, 5 large stars, and 6 small stars. See pages 35 and 39 for tree. See page 35 for tree trunk.

Directions

Use ¼" seam allowance unless otherwise noted.

See pages 73–74 for appliqué instructions.

CENTER BACKGROUND & TREE APPLIQUÉ

Placement of background & tree pieces

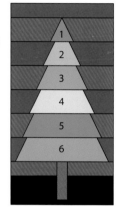

1. Trace tree pieces #1 and #2 to fusible web.

2. For pieces #3–#6, cut 5½"-wide strips of fusible web 13", 16", 19", and 23" long. Fold the pieces in half as shown, place the pattern for piece #2 on the fold, and use a rotary ruler to measure and cut the pieces.

For #3 fusible web piece for tree, place Pattern 2 on 13" folded fusible web. Place rotary ruler over pattern with 1½" line along edge of pattern. Cut fusible web.

For #4 (#5, #6), cut 3" (4½", 6") from edge of pattern.

3. For the trunk, draw a 2¼" × 8¾" rectangle on fusible web. Cut out the piece leaving a narrow margin. Fuse web to wrong side of tree trunk fabric. Cut on drawn line.

> ★ **OPTIONAL:** *To make the tree less stiff, cut out the centers of the fusible web pieces, leaving 1" or so along all the edges.*
>
>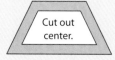
>
> Cut out center.

4. Fuse the web pieces to the wrong sides of the tree fabrics. Cut them out at the edge of the fusible web.

5. Crease the center of each tree background piece and each tree piece. Matching centers, appliqué the tree pieces to the backgrounds as shown. Stitch the bottom 2 background pieces together, then center the trunk and appliqué. Stitch all the rows together. Press the seams open.

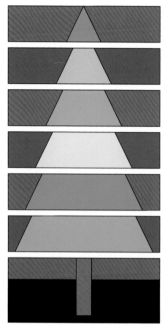

Appliqué tree pieces and trunk to backgrounds; stitch rows together.

BORDER 1

1. Stitch the Border 1 strips end to end. Press.

2. Cut 2 strips to the same length as the quilt center panel. Stitch them to the sides of the quilt. Repeat for the top and the bottom. Press.

BORDER 2

1. Make each side border by alternately stitching 11 black and 11 white squares together. Press.

2. Stitch the borders to the sides of the quilt. Repeat for the top and bottom borders using 7 black and 7 white squares in each.

GIFTS & STARS APPLIQUÉ

Appliqué the gifts and stars in the center panel.

BORDER 3

Repeat Border 1.

BORDER 4

1. Repeat Border 1.

2. Appliqué a large star to each corner, overlapping Border 3 slightly.

FINISHING

1. Cut the backing so it is the same size as the batting.

2. Layer, baste, and quilt.

3. Trim the backing and batting to the same size as the quilt top.

4. Bind the quilt using a ⅜" seam allowance (see page 78).

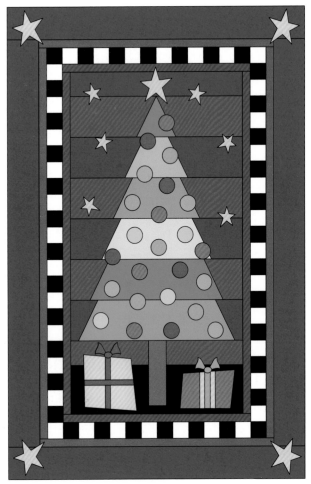

Quilt Assembly Diagram

ORNAMENTS

Patterns are on page 39–40.

1. Make a plastic template of the circle pattern. For the front of the ornament, use the template to draw a circle on the right side of one of each set of 2 squares.

2. Using a lightbox, trace the numerals, centered, inside the circles.

3. Using an appliqué pressing sheet to protect the ironing board, fuse craft-weight interfacing squares to the wrong sides of the ornament fronts.

4. Use a narrow machine zigzag to stitch the numerals.

5. Cut out each front/interfacing on the line. Cut 24 pieces of ribbon approximately 2" long (make sure the ribbon length works with the buttons or bells). Place the front/interfacing in the center of the wrong side of the backing. Place the ribbon loop at the top of the ornament between the fusible and the backing. Fuse the backing to the ornament, catching the ends of the ribbon in the fusing.

6. Fold the ribbon out of the way, and trim the backing even with the front/interfacing.

7. Machine satin stitch (close-together zigzag) outside the edge of the ornament.

8. Stitch buttons or bells to the tree using the photo and the Quilt Assembly Diagram as a guide for placement. Hang all the ornaments on the tree with the numeral side facing up, starting at the top of the tree with numeral 1.

As each day in December passes, turn over an ornament—counting backward so the blank side shows, leaving the number of days until Christmas showing.

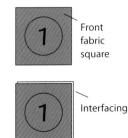 Front fabric square

Interfacing

 Cut out.

 Fuse back.

 Trim backing.

 Zigzag edge

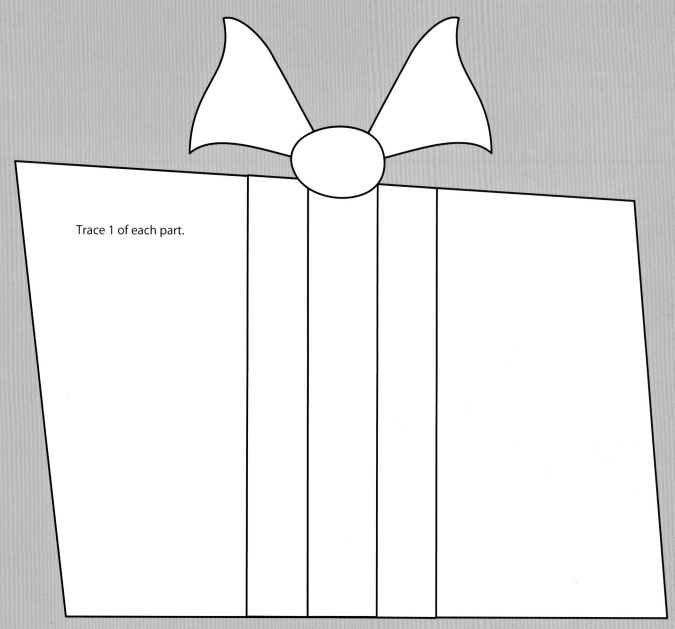

Trace 1 of each part.

Patterns are for fusible web appliqué—
they are reversed for tracing and do not
have added seam allowances.

Trace 1 of each part.

Patterns are for fusible web appliqué—
they are reversed for tracing and do not
have added seam allowances.

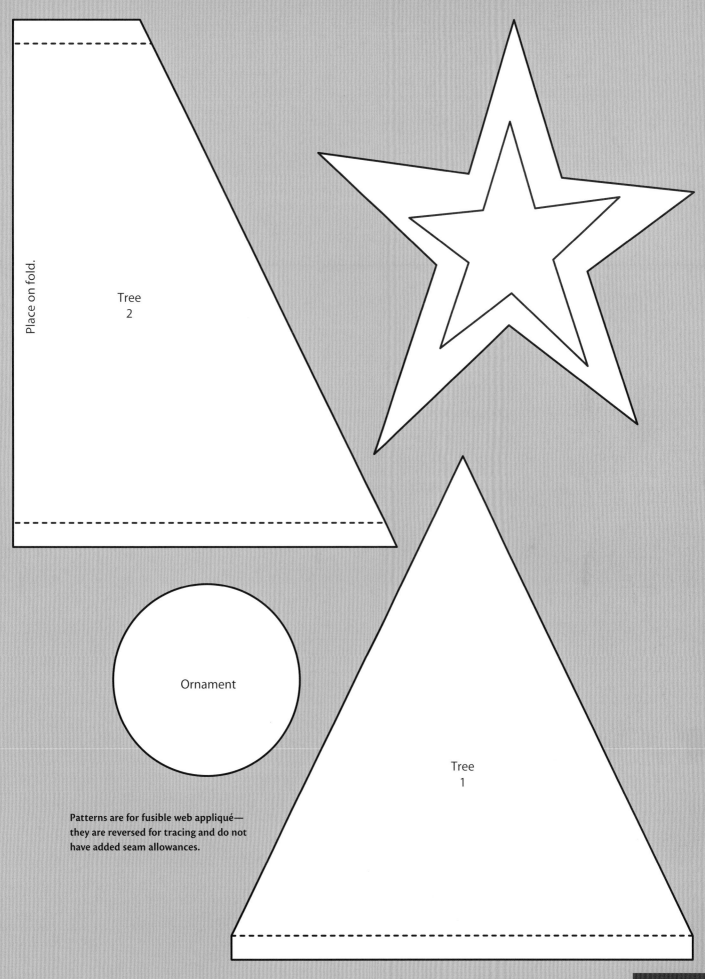

Place on fold.

Tree
2

Ornament

Tree
1

Patterns are for fusible web appliqué—
they are reversed for tracing and do not
have added seam allowances.

1 2 3 4 5
6 7 8 9 10
11 12 13 14
15 16 17 18
19 20 21 22
23 24

CHRISTMAS WITH POSSIBILITIES

Santa
place mats & casserole carrier

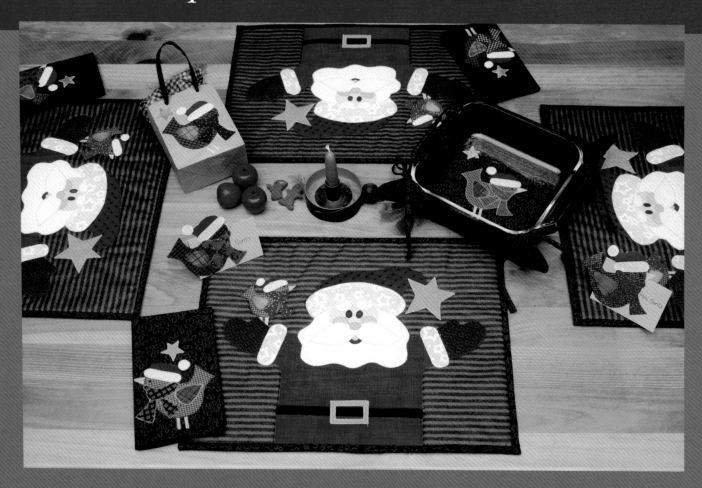

SANTA
PLACE MATS

Finished place mat size: 14″ × 18″

Materials and Yardage for Two Place Mats

Yardage is based on fabric that is at least 42″ wide.

- **Main fabric:** ½ yard
- **Fabric scraps for appliqué:** up to 7″ × 9½″
- **Backing:** ½ yard
- **Binding:** ⅜ yard
- **Batting:** 2 rectangles 16″ × 20″
- **Fusible web**

Cutting

When strips appear in the cutting list, cut crossgrain strips (selvage to selvage).

Main fabric: 2 rectangles 14″ × 18″

Backing: 2 rectangles 16″ × 20″

Binding: 4 strips 2½″ wide

Cut appliqué as needed (Patterns are on page 44.)

Note: Enlarge patterns 150%.

Directions

Use ¼″ seam allowance unless otherwise noted.

See pages 73–74 for appliqué instructions.

APPLIQUÉ

Appliqué Santa on the main fabric rectangle. Line up the raw bottom edge of the suit with the bottom edge of the rectangle so it will be caught in the binding.

FINISHING

1. Layer, baste, and quilt.

2. Trim the backing to the same size as the batting.

3. Bind the place mats using a ⅜″ seam allowance (see page 78).

SANTA
CASSEROLE CARRIER

Casserole carrier: fits an 8″ × 8″ dish

Materials and Yardage

Yardage is based on fabric that is at least 42″ wide.

Prewash fabric and batting so carrier will fit after laundering.

- **Fabric:** 1⅛ yards
- **Batting*:** 1 square 15″ × 15″
- **Heavy cardboard:** 1 square 7¼″ × 7¼″, 4 pieces 2″ × 7¼″

    *Insulating batting is available and is perfect for this project.

Cutting

Fabric

   Base: 1 square 15″ × 15″ and 1 square 14″ × 14″

   Center pocket: 1 piece 9″ × 9½″

   Side pockets: 4 pieces 6″ × 9″

   Ties: 8 pieces 1½″ × 12″

Directions

Use ¼" seam allowance unless otherwise noted.

1. Layer in order and pin: batting square, 15" × 15" fabric square right side up, and 14" × 14" fabric square right side down, and centered.

2. Stitch around the smaller square with a ⅜" seam allowance, leaving 4" open on one side for turning. Trim the large square even with the small square. Clip the corners, and turn through the opening so the batting is sandwiched between the fabric layers. Press. Pin the opening closed, and topstitch very close to the entire outside edge of the carrier.

3. Lightly mark a diagonal 2" grid on the outside of the carrier, and machine quilt on the lines.

4. Mark the fold lines on the inside of the carrier 2½" from each side.

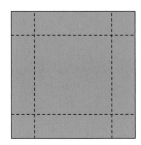

Mark fold lines.

5. To hem one 9" side of the center pocket piece: Press ½" to the wrong side, then press ½" to the wrong side again. Stitch close to the fold. The pocket should measure 8½" high by 9" wide.

6. Place the pocket wrong side down on the inside of the carrier, matching the hemmed edge with one marked fold line. Tuck under and pin 3 raw edges to meet the marked fold lines on the carrier. Press the pocket. Stitch the pinned edges very close to the folds.

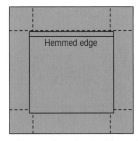

Place hemmed pocket inside carrier.

7. Press the ties in half lengthwise, wrong sides together. Unfold. Press the long raw edges in to meet the pressed line. Fold in one end, then refold along the center line. Stitch across the end and along the double-folded edge.

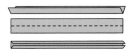

Press and stitch ties.

8. Press the side pockets in half lengthwise, wrong sides together, to 3" × 9". Place one side pocket on the side of the carrier with the fold next to the edge of the center pocket. Tuck under and pin the 3 raw edges to meet the marked fold lines and on the outside edge of the carrier. Press the pocket. Repeat for the other 3 side pockets.

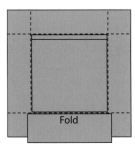

Place side pockets.

9. Tuck the raw end of a tie under the corner of the side pocket at each corner of the carrier. Pin in place. Stitch the pinned edges of the pockets, catching the ties in the stitching.

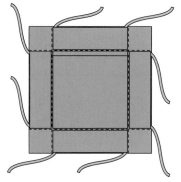

Stitch pockets, catching ties.

10. Trim the cardboard pieces slightly, if necessary, to fit the pockets. Slide the cardboard into the pockets. Fold up the sides of carrier, and tie each corner in a bow.

⭐ **OPTIONAL:** *Add appliqués to the carrier, or use the appliqués to decorate napkins, gift bags, or boxes, or use as place-card holders.*

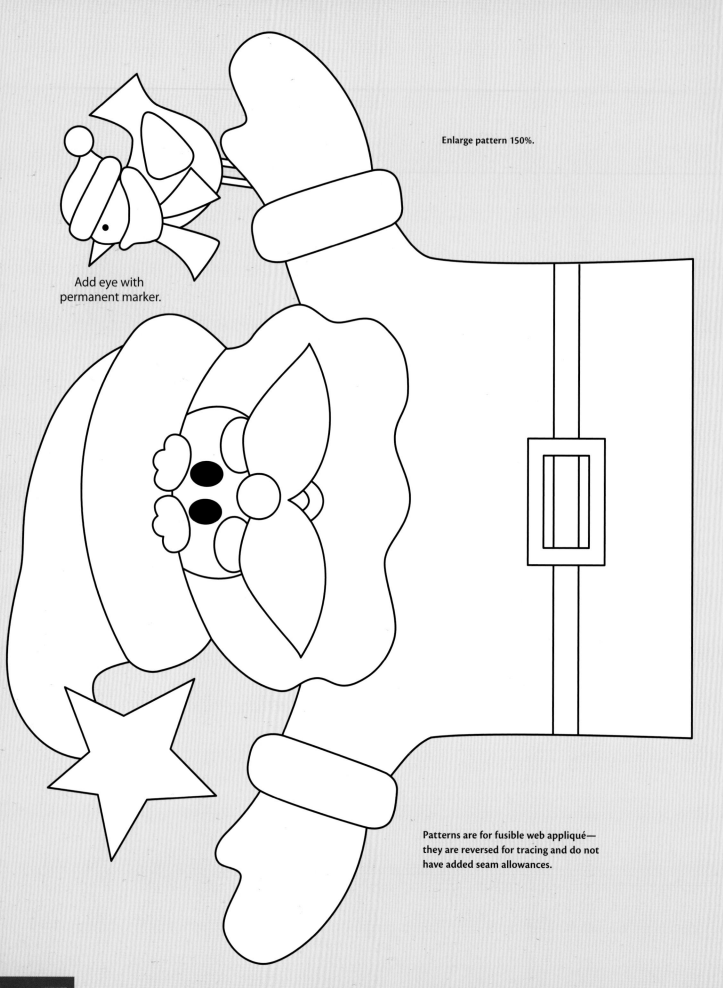

Add eye with
permanent marker.

Enlarge pattern 150%.

Patterns are for fusible web appliqué—
they are reversed for tracing and do not
have added seam allowances.

Poinsettia & Holly
table setting

POINSETTIA & HOLLY
PLACE MATS

Finished place mat size: 14″ × 18″

Place Mats

Materials and Yardage for Two Place Mats

Yardage is based on fabric that is at least 42″ wide.

- **Prequilted muslin:** ½ yard
- **Red and green scraps:** up to 3″ × 5″
- **Backing:** ½ yard
- **Binding:** ⅜ yard
- **Fusible web**

Cutting

When strips appear in the cutting list, cut crossgrain strips (selvage to selvage).

Muslin: 2 rectangles 14″ × 18″

Backing: 2 rectangles 14″ × 18″

Binding: 4 strips 2½″ wide

Cut appliqué as needed (Patterns are on page 48): 7 petals, 6 circles, and 2 holly leaves for each poinsettia **OR** 3 holly leaves and 3 berries for each holly cluster.

Directions

Use ¼″ seam allowance unless otherwise noted.

See pages 73–74 for appliqué instructions.

1. Appliqué a poinsettia or holly cluster to the top left corner of each prequilted muslin rectangle.

2. Layer a place mat front wrong sides together with a backing rectangle, and pin the edges.

3. Bind the place mats using ⅜″ seam allowance (see page 78).

POINSETTIA & HOLLY
POT HOLDERS

Finished pot holder size: 8″ × 8″

Materials and Yardage for Two Pot Holders

Yardage is based on fabric that is at least 42″ wide.

- **Prequilted muslin:** ⅓ yard
- **Red and green scraps:** up to 3″ × 5″
- **Backing:** ⅓ yard
- **Binding:** ¼ yard
- **Batting (dense cotton or insulating batting):** 2 squares 8″ × 8″
- **Fusible web**

Cutting

When strips appear in the cutting list, cut crossgrain strips (selvage to selvage).

Muslin and backing: 2 squares each 8″ × 8″

Cut appliqué as needed: see place mat cutting at left

Binding: 2 strips 2½″ wide

Directions

Use the Place Mat Directions placing the batting between the pot holder front and backing when layering.

POINSETTIA & HOLLY
TABLE RUNNER

Finished table runner size: 14" × 54"

Table Runner

Material and Yardage

Yardage is based on fabric that is at least 42" wide.

- **Prequilted muslin:** 1⅝ yards
- **Red and green scraps:** up to 3" × 5"
- **Backing:** ⅞ yard
- **Binding:** ⅜ yard
- **Green fusible bias tape:** 1½ yards
- **Fusible web**

Cutting

When strips appear in the cutting list, cut crossgrain strips (selvage to selvage).

Muslin: 1 rectangle 14" × 54"

Backing: 2 strips 14" wide

Binding: 4 strips 2½" wide

Cut appliqué as needed (patterns are on page 48):
21 poinsettia petals, 21 circles, 14 holly leaves, and 18 berries

Directions

Use ¼" seam allowance unless otherwise noted.

See pages 73–74 for appliqué instructions.

1. Pin the fusible bias tape in a gentle curve along the center of the muslin rectangle. Trim the bias tape so it ends 6" from each end of table runner.

2. Place 3 poinsettias, holly leaves, and berries along the stem as desired. Appliqué.

3. Piece the backing to 14" × 54". Layer the runner wrong sides together with the backing, and pin the edges.

4. Bind the table runner with ⅜" seam allowance (see page 78).

POINSETTIA & HOLLY
APRON

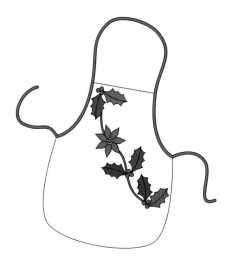

Yardage and Materials

- **Purchased or premade apron**
- **Fabric scraps for appliqué**
- **Green fusible bias tape for stem**

Cutting

Cut appliqué pieces as desired using the photo as guide. Patterns are on page 48.

Directions

Appliqué the apron using the photo and diagram as guides for placement. Use fusible bias tape for the stem.

★ *To make the cookie caddy, follow the instructions for making the casserole carrier on pages 42–43.*

Cookie Caddy

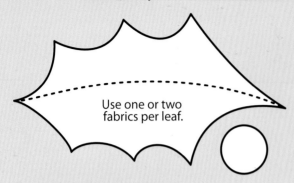

Use one or two fabrics per leaf.

Poinsettia Petal

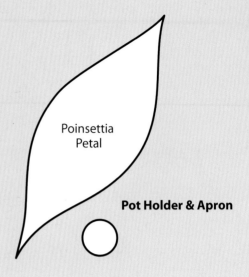

Patterns are for fusible web appliqué—they are reversed for tracing and do not have added seam allowances.

Pot Holder & Apron

Apron, Place Mat, Pot Holder, Table Runner

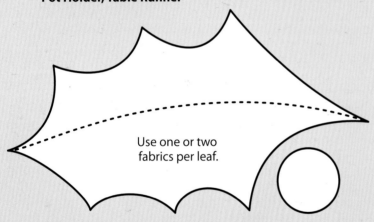

Use one or two fabrics per leaf.

Table Runner & Place Mat

Poinsettia Petal

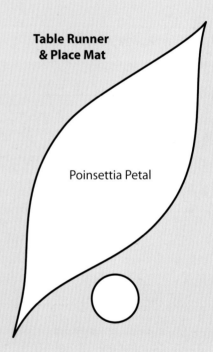

Tyrolean Christmas
quilt, table runner & place mats

TYROLEAN CHRISTMAS QUILT

Finished quilt size: 31″ × 31″

Materials and Yardage

Yardage is based on fabric that is at least 42″ wide.

- **Background:** ¼ yard each 6 creams
- **Appliqué:** ⅛ yard each 3 greens and 4 reds
- **Border 1:** ⅛ yard red
- **Border 2:** ¼ yard dark green
- **Corner triangles:** ½ yard green
- **Binding:** ⅜ yard
- **Backing:** 1¼ yards
- **Batting:** 35″ × 35″
- **Fusible web**

Cutting

When strips appear in the cutting list, cut crossgrain strips (selvage to selvage).

Background

Creams: 24 squares 2″ × 2″ of each fabric; 2 squares 2⅜″ × 2⅜″, cut each 2⅜″ square in half diagonally

Red and green: 1 square 2⅜″ × 2⅜″, cut in half diagonally from one red and one green fabric.

Border 1: 2 strips 1″ wide

Border 2: 3 strips 2″ wide

Corner triangles: 2 squares 12⅞″ × 12⅞″, cut each in half diagonally

Binding: 4 strips 2½″ wide

Cut appliqué as needed: (Patterns are on pages 53–54): 4 large flowers, 4 tall flowers, 8 hearts, and 32 triangles.

Directions

Use ¼″ seam allowance unless otherwise noted.

See pages 73–74 for appliqué instructions.

QUILT CENTER

1. Make 12 Nine-Patch blocks. Press.

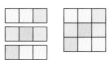

Make 12.

2. Make 4 center blocks as shown. Press.

Make 2.   Make 2.

3. Stitch the blocks into horizontal rows. Stitch the rows together. Press.

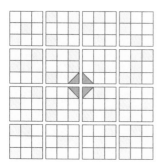 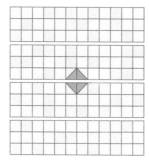

Stitch blocks together. Stitch rows together.

BORDERS AND CORNERS

1. To make Border 1: Cut 2 side borders to fit the quilt. Stitch the borders to the quilt. Repeat at the top and bottom.

2. Repeat for Border 2. Press.

3. For the corners, center and stitch 1 triangle to each side. Press.

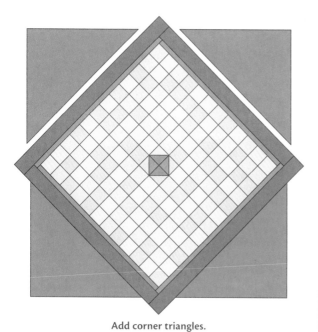

Add corner triangles.

APPLIQUÉ

Appliqué the flowers, hearts, and triangles to the quilt.

FINISHING

1. Cut the backing so it is the same size as the batting.

2. Layer, baste, and quilt.

3. Trim the excess backing and batting.

4. Bind the quilt using a ⅜" seam allowance (see page 78).

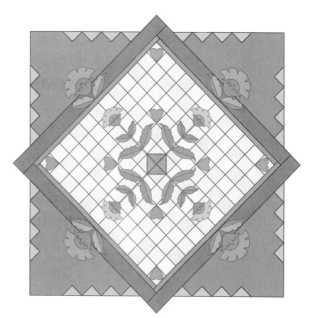

Quilt Assembly Diagram

TYROLEAN CHRISTMAS TABLE RUNNER

Finished table runner size:
12″ × 42″

Materials and Yardage

Yardage is based on fabric that is at least 42″ wide.

- **Background:** ⅜ yard each green and black

- **Squares:** ⅛ yard each light red and medium red

- **Appliqué:** ⅛ yard each 3 reds and 2 greens

- **Binding:** ⅓ yard

- **Backing:** 1⅜ yards

- **Batting:** 16″ × 46″

- **Fusible web**

Cutting

When strips appear in the cutting list, cut crossgrain strips (selvage to selvage).

Background:

  Green: 1 piece 9½″ × 28½″

  Black: 2 pieces 2″ × 28½″, 2 pieces 5½″ × 12½″

Squares: 6 squares 2½″ of each fabric

Binding: 3 strips 2½″ wide

Cut appliqué as needed (Patterns are on page 54): 6 tall flowers, omit large leaves, and shorten stems to 2¾″.

Directions

Use ¼″ seam allowance unless otherwise noted.

See pages 73–74 for appliqué instructions.

APPLIQUÉ

Appliqué 3 flowers to each 5½″ × 12½″ black rectangle, extending the stem, but not the leaves, into seam allowance.

ASSEMBLE THE RUNNER TOP

1. Stitch the long black pieces to the green piece. Stitch the short black pieces to each end, with the stems of the flowers facing. Press.

2. Stitch the red squares into 2 units of 6, alternating fabrics. Press. Stitch them to the ends of the table runner. Press.

FINISHING

1. Cut the backing so it is the same size as the batting.

2. Layer, baste, and quilt.

3. Trim the backing and batting to the same size as the quilt top.

4. Bind the quilt using a ⅜″ seam allowance (see page 78).

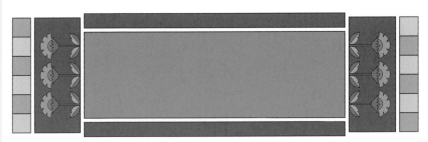

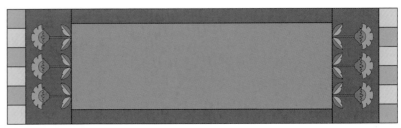

Runner Assembly Diagram

TYROLEAN CHRISTMAS PLACE MATS

Finished place mat size: 14″ × 18″

Materials and Yardage for Four Place Mats

Yardage is based on fabric that is at least 42″ wide.

- **Prequilted fabric:** 1 yard

- **Appliqué:** ⅛ yard each of 2 reds and ¼ yard each of 2 greens

- **Binding:** ⅞ yard

Cutting

When strips appear in the cutting list, cut crossgrain strips (selvage to selvage).

Prequilted fabric: 4 pieces 14″ × 18″

Binding: 8 strips 3¼″ wide

Cut appliqué as needed (Patterns are on page 54): 8 tall flowers, shorten stems to 3¾″.

Directions

Use ¼″ seam allowance unless otherwise noted.

See pages 73–74 for appliqué instructions.

1. Appliqué 2 flowers on the right side of each place mat, keeping pieces ¾″–1″ from the edge.

2. Bind the place mat with a ½″ seam allowance (see page 78). Repeat for the other place mats.

Place Mat

Patterns are for fusible web appliqué—they are reversed for tracing and do not have added seam allowances.

Patterns are for fusible web appliqué—they are reversed
for tracing and do not have added seam allowances.

Christmas
album cover

Photo by C&T Publishing

CHRISTMAS
ALBUM COVER

Materials and Yardage

Yardage is based on fabric that is at least 42" wide.

- **Oversized 3-ring binder made especially for scrapbooks** (approximately 11½" tall by 12½" wide*)

- **Cover fabric:** ½ yard **OR** 1⅛ yards if fabric is directional

- **Fabric scraps for appliqués**

- **Heavy or craft-weight iron-on interfacing:** 1⅛ yards

- **Optional:** spray fabric protector**

- **Fusible web:** 1 yard

*The binders we like best are oversized to protect the edges of pages, usually have D-rings, and fold back at the spine.

**We recommend spraying all fabrics before using a fabric protector such as Scotchgard.

Directions

Use ¼" seam allowance unless otherwise noted.

Appliqué patterns are on pages 58–59.

See pages 73–74 for appliqué instructions.

1. Place the interfacing adhesive side down on a table. Place the open binder on the interfacing, centering it from end to end and top to bottom.

2. Mark around the binder on the interfacing with a pen or pencil. Hold the pen/pencil upright while marking. Mark 4 short vertical lines to show the position of the spine. Remove the binder.

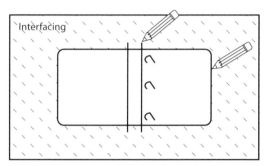

Mark around binder on interfacing.

3. Connect the short vertical marks to complete the spine position markings. To mark the cutting line, make a line outside the binder line that is 1" from each long side and 5" from each short side. Cut out the interfacing on the cutting line.

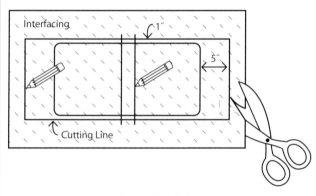

Cut out interfacing.

4. Cut a piece of cover fabric 2" bigger in each direction than the interfacing. Center the fusible side of the interfacing on the wrong side of the cover fabric. Fuse the interfacing to the fabric, following the manufacturer's directions. Cut off the excess fabric to match the interfacing.

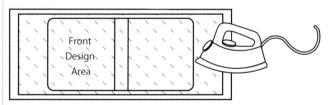

Fuse interfacing to cover fabric.

5. On all the edges, fold ¼" to the wrong side and stitch, forming a hem.

6. Transfer the front edge line to the right side of the cover by placing pins end to end on the right side. Transfer the front spine line to the right side of the cover in the same way. The space between the pin lines is the front design area.

Create front design area.

7. Cut out and fuse background pieces and appliqués. Do not put the spine label on at this time. Note that ¾" at top and bottom will be lost in the facing.

> ★ **NOTE:** *To line white or very light fabrics, fuse to a layer of white fabric with fusible web, then fuse the traced pattern to the white lining.*

8. Appliqué background pieces to front design area. Appliqué Santa and other shapes to backgrounds.

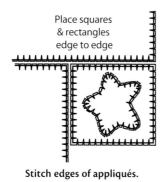

Stitch edges of appliqués.

9. Fold over the front end of the cover, right sides together, along the penciled front edge line. Machine baste ⅛"–¼" outside the top and bottom binder lines. Turn the cover

right side out; and try it on the binder so adjustments can be made. The cover should fit snugly. Adjust the seams if necessary. Restitch with a normal stitch length. Repeat the basting for the back edge of the cover. If the binder is particularly thick, the back edge line may have to be moved out about ¼" as shown. When the correct fit is established, restitch with a normal stitch length.

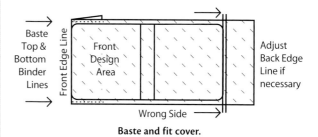

Baste and fit cover.

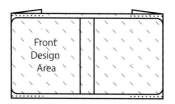

Stitch cover with normal stitch length.

10. Turn the cover right side out. Finger-press to the inside the facing formed at the top and bottom edges.

Finger-press facing.

11. Put the cover on the binder. Center the spine letters and/or the background rectangle on the spine. Fuse it to the cover. Remove the cover, and appliqué.

12. Open the binder, and slide the front and back edges of the binder into the cover.

Patterns are for fusible web appliqué—
they are reversed for tracing and do not
have added seam allowances.

Cut candle square 2″ × 2″

Cut candy rectangle 2″ × 4″

Cut stocking rectangle 2″ × 3″

Use permanent marker for Santa's
eyes and sleeve lines.

Cut Santa
rectangle 6″ × 8″,
then cut out 2″ × 5″
from top left corner

CHRISTMAS

Cut Christmas rectangle 2″ × 7″

Use same lettering & rectangle for spine.

Cut reindeer rectangle 5″ × 5″

Cut tree rectangle 3″ × 5″

**Patterns are for fusible web appliqué—
they are reversed for tracing and do not
have added seam allowances.**

Use permanent marker for reindeer eye and bell centers.

Eco Friendly
bags

Photo by C&T Publishing

ECO FRIENDLY
TOTE

Finished tote size: 14″ w × 14″ h × 6″ d

Materials and Yardage

Yardage is based on fabric that is at least 42″ wide.

- **Main fabric:** ⅔ yard
- **Lining, inside binding:** ¾ yard
- **Pockets:** ⅜ yard
- **Trim:** ¼ yard
- **Handles, pocket binding:** ⅝ yard
- **Batting**

    Bag: 19″ × 42″

Pockets: 2 pieces 8″ × 10″

Handles: 2 pieces 2⅜″ × 53″

■ **Cardboard, matboard, or thin Masonite:** 6″ × 14″ (optional)

Cutting

When strips appear in the cutting list, cut crossgrain strips (selvage to selvage).

Main fabric: 19″ × 42″

Lining

  Bag: 19″ × 42″

  Binding: 2 strips 1½″ wide

Pockets: 2 pieces 10″ × 16″

Trim: 1 strip 5″ wide

Handles: 3 strips 5″ wide

Pocket binding: 1 strip 2½″ wide

Directions

Use ¼″ seam allowance unless otherwise noted.

1. Layer the lining, bag batting, and main fabric. Quilt in parallel lines. Cut the quilted rectangle to 18″ × 41″.

2. Place the trim on the lining side of the bag, right sides together and raw edges even, and stitch. Press ¼″ to the wrong side on the unstitched long edge of the trim. Turn the trim to the outside of the bag, press, and topstitch the folded edge of the trim to the bag. Quilt the trim in horizontal lines.

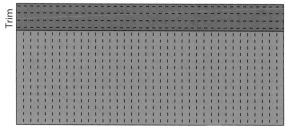

Quilt bag.

3. Press the pocket pieces in half, wrong sides together, to 8″ × 10″. The fold is the bottom of the pocket. Slide the batting between the layers. Quilt the pockets diagonally in both directions or as desired. Trim the edges even. Press the pocket binding in half lengthwise, wrong sides together. Bind just the top edges of the pockets. Make 2 pockets.

4. Stitch the handle strips end to end, and cut 2 pieces 54″ long. For each handle, place the batting on the wrong side of the fabric rectangle, centered from side to side. Press the short fabric ends over the batting. Press the long edges of the fabric over the batting to meet in the center. Fold the strip in half lengthwise and press. Pin and topstitch close to all the edges. Topstitch again ¼″ inside the first line of stitching.

5. Pin the pockets and the handles to the bag as shown, with the handles covering the raw side edges of the pockets. Stitch close to the lower edge of the pocket and again ¼″ away. Topstitch along the previous stitching lines on the handles, stopping at the lower edge of the trim.

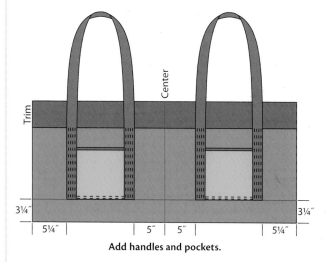

Add handles and pockets.

6. Fold the bag in half along the center line, right sides together. Stitch the side and bottom edges. Using a 1½″ strip of single thickness, bind the seam allowance of the side and bottom.

7. With the bag turned wrong side out, fold the bottom corners of the bag, with the side of the bag matched to the bottom seam. Mark the box-bottom seams 3″ from the point as shown. Stitch on the marked lines. Tack the triangles to the bottom seam. Turn right side out.

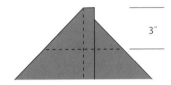

Measure and stitch box-bottom seams.

8. OPTIONAL INSERT: For a rigid bottom, cut cardboard, matboard, or Masonite 6″ × 14″. Cover it with fabric or fabric and thin batting if desired.

ECO FRIENDLY
LUNCH BAG

Finished lunch bag size: 7″ w × 9″ h × 4″ d

Materials and Yardage

Yardage is based on fabric that is at least 42″ wide.

- **Main fabric:** ½ yard

- **Lining, inside binding:** ½ yard

- **Trim:** ⅛ yard

- **Handles:** ¼ yard

- **Batting**

   Bag: 13″ × 24″

   Handles: 2 pieces 2⅜″ × 18″

- **Cardboard, matboard, or thin Masonite:** 4″ × 7″ (optional)

Cutting

When strips appear in the cutting list, cut crossgrain strips (selvage to selvage).

Main fabric: 13″ × 24″

Lining

   Bag: 13″ × 24″

   Binding: 1 strip 1½″

Trim: 3″ × 23″

Handles: 2 pieces 5″ × 19″

Directions

Use ¼″ seam allowance unless otherwise noted.

Follow the directions for the Eco Friendly Tote but with the following exceptions:

Step 1: Cut the quilted rectangle to 12″ × 23″.

Step 3: Skip this step.

Steps 4/5: Make the handles as described, using the 2⅜″ × 18″ strips, and attach to the bag as shown below.

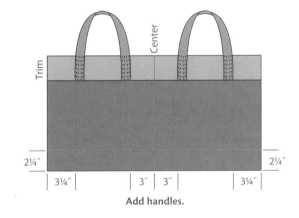

Add handles.

Step 7: Make the box bottom as described, marking the seams 2″ from the point as shown.

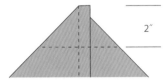

Measure and stitch box-bottom seams.

Step 8: Cut the optional insert to 4″ × 7″.

ECO FRIENDLY
WINE BAG

Finished wine bag size: 3½″ w × 18″ h × 3½″ d

Materials and Yardage

Yardage is based on fabric that is at least 42″ wide.

- **Main fabric:** ½ yard
- **Lining fabric:** ½ yard
- **Ribbons:** 1 yard each of 1 or more colors
- **Cardboard, matboard, or thin Masonite:** 3½″ × 3½″

Cutting

Main fabric: 20″ × 15″

Lining: 20″ × 15″

Directions

Use ¼″ seam allowance unless otherwise noted.

1. Place the main fabric and the lining pieces right sides together, and stitch one 15″ side. Press the seam allowance toward the lining.

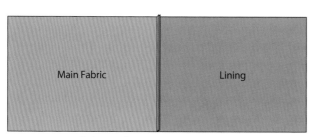

Stitch together main fabric and lining.

2. Fold the piece in half, right sides together, to 39½″ × 7½″. Stitch the raw edges, leaving an opening on the lining side for turning. Turn right side out through the opening, and push the lining into the main fabric. Press.

Leave opening for turning.

Top edge with lining on inside

3. Turn the bag wrong side out. Fold each bottom corner, with the center side of the bag matched to the bottom seam, and mark the box-bottom seam 1¾″ from the point. Stitch on the marked lines. Tack the triangles to the bottom seam. Turn the bag right side out.

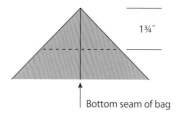

1¾″

Bottom seam of bag

4. If you are using the optional insert, cover the cardboard, mat board, or Masonite with fabric if desired. Insert it into the bottom of the wine bag.

5. Place a wine bottle in the bag, turn the top of the bag approximately 2″ to the outside, forming a cuff. Tie a ribbon around the neck of the bottle, and trim the length of the ribbon as desired.

Reindeer & Santa
pillows

Photo by C&T Publishing

Finished pillow size: 14″ × 14″ plus button flange

Materials and Yardage for 1 Pillow

Yardage is based on fabric that is at least 42″ wide.

- **Pillow cover:** ¾ yard

- **Appliqué square:** ⅜ yard

- **Accent square:** ⅜ yard

- **Medium and small scraps for appliqué**

- **Pillow buttons:** (4) ¾″–1″ (Jingle bells are an alternative)

- **Patch buttons:** (4) ½″–¾″

- **14″ × 14″ pillow form**

- **Fusible web**

Cutting

Pillow cover: 21½″ × 30½″

Appliqué square: 1 square 10½″ × 10½″

Accent square: 2 squares 11½″ × 11½″

Cut appliqué as needed (Patterns are on pages 66–67.)

Pillow Cover

Use ¼″ seam allowance unless otherwise noted.

See pages 73–74 for appliqué instructions.

1. Press a 2″ hem to the wrong side of one 30½″ side of the pillow cover. Press 2″ to the wrong side again, forming a hem of double thickness.

2. Open the pressed hem. Fold the pillow cover in half with the right sides together, matching the 21½″ sides. Stitch as shown. Turn right side out. Press.

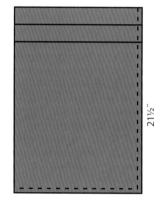

21½″

Fold pillow cover in half, and stitch.

3. Refold the pressed hem, and pin it in place. Stitch the hem close to the fold.

4. Make 4 buttonholes on top of the hem placed 3″ apart (3″-6″-9″-12″). Stitch the buttons in position so they align with the buttonholes.

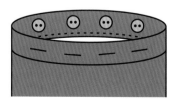

Add buttons and buttonholes.

Appliqué and Accent Patches

1. Apply fusible web to wrong side of the 10½″ appliqué square, then trim to a 10″ square. To the right side of one accent square, center and fuse appliqué square. Appliqué with a narrow zigzag or buttonhole stitch.

2. Appliqué the pieces to the appliqué square.

> ★ *To line white or very light fabrics, fuse the wrong side of the appliqué fabric to white lining fabric first, then fuse the traced pattern to the wrong side of the new double-thick fabric.*

Accent Square

Appliqué Square

3. Place the accent squares right sides together. Stitch around the entire square leaving about 2″ open for turning. Clip the corners, turn the square right side out, and press. Slipstitch the opening closed.

Finishing

1. Attach the square to the pillow cover by stitching buttons at each corner through all layers.

> ★ **OPTIONAL:** *To make the patch removable, make buttonholes in the corners of the squares, and sew buttons to the pillow cover under the buttonholes.*

Patterns are for fusible web appliqué—
they are reversed for tracing and do not
have added seam allowances.

Patterns are for fusible web appliqué—
they are reversed for tracing and do not
have added seam allowances.

Use a fine-point permanent marker
for eyes and powder blush applied
with a cotton swab for cheeks.

Santa *stockings*

Finished stocking length: 20″

Materials and Yardage for One Stocking

Yardage is based on fabric that is at least 42″ wide.

- **Stocking and lining:** ¾ yard
- **Scraps for appliqués:** up to 4″ × 11″ and 5″ × 6″
- **Binding:** ⅓ yard
- **Batting:** 14″ × 22″
- **Fusible web**

Cutting

Note: Enlarge stocking pattern (page 69) 200% before cutting.

Stocking and lining: 2 stockings and 2 reversed

Binding: 2½″ wide (on the bias), pieced to 70″ long

Batting: 1 piece using pattern

Cut appliqué as needed (Patterns are on pages 69–72.)

Note: Enlarge Santas 120% before tracing.

Directions

Use ¼" seam allowance unless otherwise noted.

See pages 73–74 for appliqué instructions.

1. Appliqué the stocking front. Reduce the letters as needed on a copier for longer names.

2. Place the stocking front and lining wrong sides together with the batting between. Baste ¼" from the outside edge. Quilt as desired. Place the stocking back and lining wrong sides together.

3. Press the binding strip in half lengthwise, wrong sides together. Bind the top edges of stocking front and back using a ⅜" seam allowance.

4. Pin the stocking front to the stocking back, lining sides together. Baste ¼" from the edge.

5. Bind the raw edges with ⅜" seam allowance, leaving a 6" tail at the top left to make a hanger. Fold the end to the inside at the top right.

6. For the hanger, stitch the folded edges of the binding tail together. Fold the raw end under on the back of the stocking, and stitch it in place.

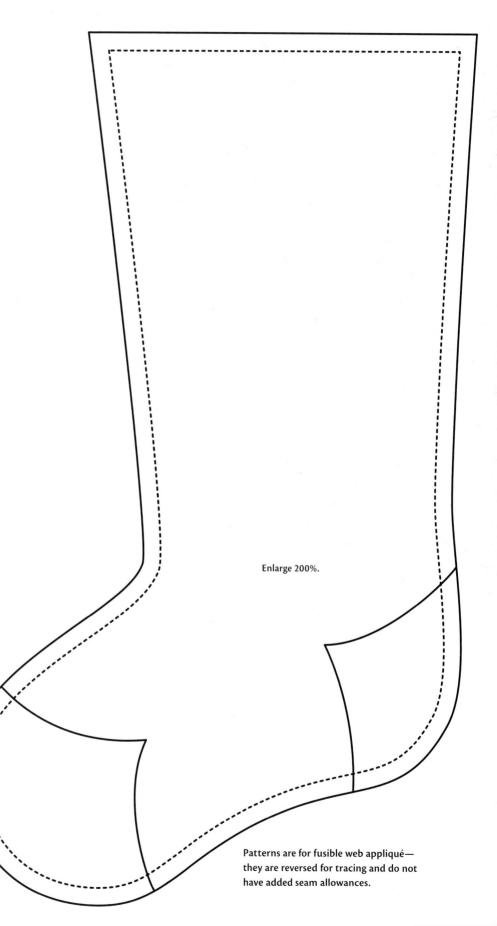

Enlarge 200%.

Patterns are for fusible web appliqué—they are reversed for tracing and do not have added seam allowances.

Use one or two fabrics per leaf.

Add eyes with permanent marker.

Enlarge 120% for Santa Stockings.

Enlarge 200% for Three Tall Santas Quilt (page 11).

Do not enlarge light bulbs, holly, or berries.

Patterns are for fusible web appliqué—they are reversed for tracing and do not have added seam allowances.

Add eyes with permanent marker.

Enlarge 120% for Santa Stockings.

Enlarge 200% for Three Tall Santas Quilt (page 11).

Do not enlarge letters.

Patterns are for fusible web appliqué—they are reversed for tracing and do not have added seam allowances.

Patterns are for fusible web appliqué—they are reversed for tracing and do not have added seam allowances.

QUILTING BASICS

Fabric

We recommend using 100% cotton fabric for making quilts. Fabric requirements are based on a 42" width, but many fabrics shrink when washed, and widths vary by manufacturer, so yardage is calculated based on 40". Prewash fabric, and check for colorfastness before using.

Seam Allowances

A ¼" seam allowance is used for most projects. It is a good idea to do a test seam before you begin stitching to check that your ¼" is accurate.

Rotary Cutting

For squares and rectangles, follow the cutting instructions for each project.

Odd-sized and asymmetrical pieces can be cut quickly with a rotary cutter. Cut around the paper pattern, making sure the pattern includes the ¼" seam allowance. Layer the fabric either by folding (which will result in original-image and reverse-image pieces) or by stacking fabric pieces with the right side up (which will result only in original-image pieces). Tape the pattern to the top layer of the fabric with a loop of tape. Use a rotary cutter and small ruler to cut around the pattern, moving the ruler as needed.

Piecing

- Be sure to use a ¼" seam allowance when stitching.

- Use a light neutral thread when stitching most fabrics. If all the fabrics are dark, use a dark thread.

- Place the pieces to be joined right sides together. Pin, matching raw edges and any seamlines, and sew with a straight stitch (10–12 stitches per inch, depending on your machine). Press the seam allowances toward the darker fabric, unless otherwise noted.

- To save time and thread, chain piece by stitching a seam and then immediately feeding in a new set of pieces without lifting the presser foot or clipping the threads. Stitch as many sets as needed, then clip them apart.

- Where two seams meet, position one seam allowance in one direction and the other seam allowance in the opposite direction. Push the seams together tightly; they will hold each other in place as you stitch. This is often called "nesting" the seams. It is usually not necessary to pin.

Nest the seams.

- When squares are cut in half on the diagonal, the cut units are called half-square triangles. When half-square triangles are stitched together, the square they form is called a half-square triangle unit because it is made from two half-square triangles. You can make half-square triangle units by cutting the given squares on the diagonal and piecing the appropriate pairs together.

Cut on diagonal.   **Stitch together.**   **Finished unit**

- When piecing, if one of the edges to be pieced appears to be larger, put that side down (next to the feed dogs), so the extra fabric will be eased into the seam without leaving tucks.

Machine Appliqué Using Fusible Web

1. Trace the patterns onto the smooth, paper side of the fusible web. Unless otherwise noted, the patterns in this book have already been reversed and are ready to be traced.

2. Use paper-cutting scissors to roughly cut out the traced pieces, adding at least ¼″ around the edges of each pattern.

3. Follow the manufacturer's instructions to iron the fusible web pieces to the wrong side of the selected appliqué fabric. Use a nonstick appliqué pressing sheet to avoid getting adhesive on your iron or ironing board.

4. Cut out the fused pieces along the traced line. Do not remove the paper until you are ready to fuse the pieces to your project.

5. When you are ready to appliqué, remove the paper, and position the appliqué piece on your project. Be sure the web (rough) side is down. Press in place, following the manufacturer's instructions. If the design is layered, arrange all the appliqué pieces before fusing.

6. The raw edges of the appliqué pieces can be finished with a satin stitch, buttonhole stitch, or zigzag stitch.

Paper Piecing

Paper piecing can be used to create very accurate blocks.

> ★ **NOTE:** *You stitch on the side of the paper with the printed lines, and place the fabric on the nonprinted side.*

1. Trace or photocopy the number of paper-piecing patterns needed.

2. Use a smaller-than-usual stitch length (1.5–1.8 or 18–20 stitches per inch, depending on your machine) and a slightly larger needle (size 90/14). This makes the paper removal easier and will result in tighter stitches that will not be pulled apart when you tear the paper off.

3. Cut the fabric pieces slightly larger than necessary— about ¾″ larger; they do not need to be perfect shapes. (One of the joys of paper piecing!)

4. Pin the first piece of fabric to the center of the block on the nonprinted side of the paper, but make sure you do not place the pin anywhere near a seamline. Hold the paper up

to the light to make sure the piece covers the area it is supposed to, with the seam allowance also amply covered.

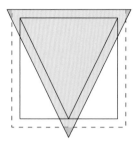

Place fabric on nonprinted side of paper.

5. Fold the pattern back at the stitching lines, and trim the fabric to a ¼″ seam allowance with a ruler and rotary cutter.

6. Cut the side triangles large enough to cover the side areas plus a generous seam allowance. It is a good idea to cut each piece larger than you think necessary; it might be a bit wasteful, but it is easier than ripping out tiny stitches! Align the edge of the side triangle with the trimmed seam allowance of the center, right sides together, and pin. With the paper side up, stitch on the line.

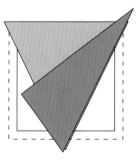

Align next piece with trimmed edge.

7. Open the side piece and press.

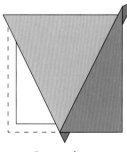

Open and press.

8. Stitch the other side triangle, and press open.

9. Trim all around the finished unit on the dashed line, leaving a ¼″ seam allowance. Leave the paper intact until after the blocks have been stitched together, then carefully remove the paper.

Finished unit

Borders

When border strips are cut crosswise, selvage to selvage, diagonally piece the strips together to achieve the needed length.

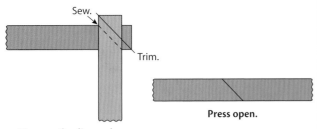

Sew.

Trim.

Piece on the diagonal.

Press open.

STAIR-STEP BORDERS

1. In most cases the side borders are stitched on first. When you have finished the quilt top, measure the length of the quilt top from cut edge to cut edge in several places. Do not measure along the edge of the quilt, as it is often stretched and will measure longer than a measurement taken through the center. Take an average of the measurements. This will be the length to cut the side borders.

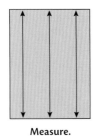

Measure.

2. Fold one side border and one side of the quilt top into quarters, and mark the folds with pins. Match the marked points, and pin the border to the quilt, right sides together. This distributes any ease along the entire edge of the quilt. Mark and pin the other side border.

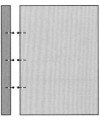

Pin the marked points.

3. Stitch the borders to the quilt, using a ¼″ seam allowance.

4. Press the seam allowances toward the outside edge of the quilt.

5. Repeat the process for the top and bottom borders.

Repeat for top and bottom borders.

MITERED CORNER BORDERS

1. Measure the length of the quilt top from seamline to seamline in several places. Do not measure along the edge of the quilt, as it is often stretched and will measure longer than a measurement taken through the center. Take an average of the measurements, and add 2 times the width of your border, plus 2″ to 4″ extra. This is the length you need to cut for the side borders.

2. Find the center of the long inside edge of one side border, and mark it with a pin. Measure from the pin in each direction, one-half the quilt length measurement, and mark with pins. These marks correspond to the corner seam intersections on the quilt top. Mark the other side border.

3. Find the center of the quilt side by folding the quilt in half, and mark the center with a pin. Pin the side border to the quilt, right sides together, matching the center and seam intersections. Mark and pin the other side border.

4. Stitch the side borders to the quilt, stopping and back-stitching at the seam intersection, ¼″ in from the edge. The excess length will extend beyond each edge. Press the seams toward the outer edge of the quilt.

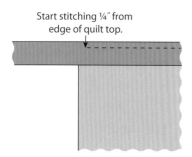

Start stitching ¼″ from edge of quilt top.

5. Repeat the process for the top and bottom borders.

6. To create the miter, lay a corner on the ironing board. Working with the quilt right side up, lay one border strip on top of the adjacent border. You may want to pin the quilt to the ironing board to keep it from slipping.

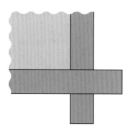

Overlap borders at corner.

7. With the borders overlapping, fold one border under at a 45° angle. Match the seams or stripes, and work with it until it matches perfectly.

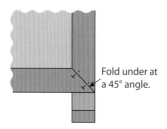

Fold under at a 45° angle.

8. Position a 90° triangle or ruler over the corner to check that the corner is flat and square. When everything is in place, press the fold firmly.

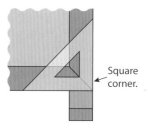

Square corner.

9. Fold the center section of the quilt top diagonally from the corner, right sides together, and align the long edges of the border strips. On the wrong side, place pins near the pressed fold in the corner to secure the border strips.

10. Beginning at the inside corner, backstitch, and then stitch along the fold toward the outside point, being careful not to allow any stretching to occur. Backstitch at the end. Trim the excess border fabric to a ¼″ seam allowance. Press the seam open.

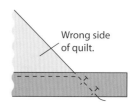

Wrong side of quilt.

Stitch toward the outside edge.

Backing

Plan on making the backing a minimum of 2″ to 3″ larger than the quilt top on all sides. For larger quilts that require pieced backings, piece the backing either horizontally or vertically; or to economize, you can piece the backing from leftover fabrics or blocks. Prewash the backing fabric, and trim the selvages before use.

Twin

Full or Double

Queen or King

Suggested vertical piecing

Batting

The type of batting to use is a personal decision; consult your local quilt shop. Cut batting at least 2" larger than your quilt top on all sides. Be sure to coordinate the density of the quilting with the batting and the design of the quilt top.

Layering

To layer the backing, batting, and quilt top, spread the backing wrong side up, and tape the edges down with masking tape. If you are working on carpet, you can use T-pins to secure the backing to the carpet. Center the batting on top, smoothing out any folds. Place the quilt top right side up on top of the batting and backing, making sure it is centered. Trim the batting to the same size as the backing, if the batting is bigger.

Basting

Basting joins the three layers (quilt top, batting, and backing) together in preparation for quilting.

If you plan to machine quilt, pin baste the quilt layers together with 1" brass or specially coated safety pins placed a minimum of 4" to 6" apart. Begin basting in the center, and move toward the edges, placing the pins where they will not be in the way of the planned quilting.

An alternative to pin basting is spray baste, which is sold in aerosol cans.

If you plan to hand quilt, baste the layers together with thread, using a long needle and light-colored thread. Knot one end of the thread. Use stitches approximately the length of the needle, and begin in the center and move out toward the edges. A sunburst design or grid pattern works well. After the quilt is basted, roll the outside edges of the backing and batting to the front of the quilt, and baste in place. This will protect the edges of the batting during quilting. As quilting stitches are added, the basting stitches can be removed.

 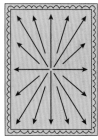

Grid pattern   **Sunburst pattern**

Quilting

Quilting, whether by hand or machine, enhances the pieced or appliqué design of the quilt. You may choose to quilt in-the-ditch, echo the pieced or appliqué motifs, use patterns from quilting design books and stencils, or do your own free-motion quilting. As mentioned previously, be sure to coordinate the density of the quilting with the batting and the design of the quilt top.

Binding

A double-fold binding is recommended because of its durability. Bias binding is not needed unless you are binding curved edges.

Trim the excess batting and backing from the quilt. For a ⅜″ finished binding, cut the binding strips 2½″ wide. For a ¼″ finished binding (used on quilts with star points at the edge), cut the binding strips 2¼″ wide. Piece the strips together as needed with a diagonal seam to make a continuous binding strip. (See page 75 for instructions on making a diagonal seam.) The diagonal seam will reduce bulk when you stitch the binding to the quilt. Press the seams open, then press the entire strip in half lengthwise with wrong sides together.

MITERED CORNERS

1. With raw edges even, pin the binding to the edge of the quilt at least 12″ away from a corner. Leave the first 6″ of the binding unattached. Start stitching, using a ¼″ or ⅜″ seam allowance as directed.

2. Stop ¼″ or ⅜″ away from the first corner. Leave the needle in the fabric, and pivot the quilt 90°. Backstitch to the edge.

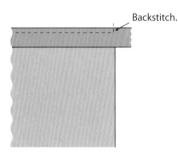

Stop and pivot quilt.

3. Lift the presser foot and needle. Pull the quilt slightly away from the machine, leaving the threads attached. Fold the binding so it extends straight above the quilt.

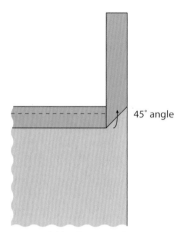

Fold binding straight up.

4. Bring the binding strip down even with the edge of the quilt. Resume stitching at the top edge.

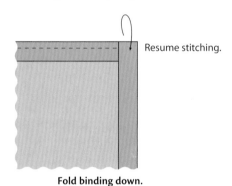

Fold binding down.

5. After making all 4 of the mitered corners, stop stitching 6″ from the beginning stitching. Take the quilt out of the sewing machine. Place the ends of the binding along the unstitched edge of the quilt. Trim the ends so they overlap by ½″.

6. Unfold the binding. Place the ends of the binding right sides together, and stitch with a ¼″ seam. Finger-press the seam open, refold the binding, and stitch the remaining binding to the quilt.

7. Turn the binding to the back of the quilt, and hand stitch the folded edge to just cover the stitched line. To distribute bulk, fold each corner miter in the opposite direction from where it was folded and stitched on the front.

ABOUT THE AUTHORS

Also by Lynda Milligan and Nancy Smith:

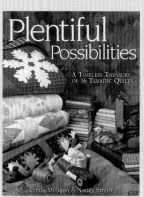

In 1981 Nancy Smith and Lynda Milligan joined forces to establish Great American Quilt Factory, Inc. The store, in Denver, Colorado, specialized in quilting patterns, fabrics, classes, and supplies. Four years later, Nancy and Lynda began designing patterns for quilts, stuffed animals, and dolls. In 1985 they formed DreamSpinners, the pattern division of Great American Quilt Factory, Inc.

In 1987, the business needed more space and moved to its present location on East Hampden Avenue in Denver. Consequently, DreamSpinners continued to grow and eventually became the largest independent pattern company in the United States.

In 1988 Nancy and Lynda created Possibilities as a book publishing division. To date, Possibilities has published more than 70 titles. In 1992 the I'll Teach Myself series was created to introduce sewing to a younger generation.

Today, Lynda and Nancy continue to maintain the retail store. They also design lines of fabric for Quilting Treasures.

Great Titles *from* C&T PUBLISHING

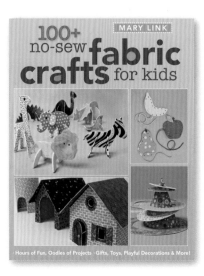

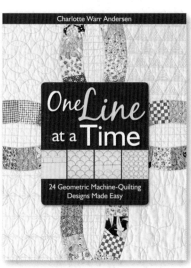

Available at your local retailer or **www.ctpub.com** *or* **800-284-1114**

For a list of other fine books from C&T Publishing, ask for a free catalog:

C&T PUBLISHING, INC.
P.O. Box 1456
Lafayette, CA 94549
800-284-1114

Email: ctinfo@ctpub.com

Website: www.ctpub.com

C&T Publishing's professional photography services are now available to the public. Visit us at www.ctmediaservices.com.

Tips and Techniques can be found at www.ctpub.com > Consumer Resources > Quiltmaking Basics: Tips & Techniques for Quiltmaking & More

For quilting supplies:

GREAT AMERICAN QUILT FACTORY - HOME OF POSSIBILITIES
8970 E. Hampden Avenue
Denver CO 80231
Store: 303-740-6206 or 800-474-2665
Website: www.greatamericanquilt.com

COTTON PATCH
1025 Brown Ave.
Lafayette, CA 94549
Store: 925-284-1177
Mail order: 925-283-7883

Email: CottonPa@aol.com

Website: www.quiltusa.com

Note: Fabrics used in the quilts shown may not be currently available, a fabric manufacturers keep most fabrics in print for only a short time.